Leadership Ex

Leadership Examined

Knowledge and Activities for Effective Practice

Colin McCall and Hugh Lawlor

London: The Stationery Office

Applications for reproduction should be made in writing to The Stationery Office Limited, St Crispins, Duke Street, Norwich NR3 1PD.

The information contained in this publication is believed to be correct at the time of manufacture. Whilst care has been taken to ensure that the information is accurate, the publisher can accept no responsibility for any errors or omissions or for changes to the details given.

A CIP catalogue record for this book is available from the British Library

First published 2000

ISBN 0 11 702612 3

Printed in the United Kingdom by Albert Gait Ltd, Grimsby
TJ2127 C10 9/00

Published by The Stationery Office and available from:

The Stationery Office
(mail, telephone and fax orders only)
PO Box 29, Norwich NR3 1GN
General enquiries/Telephone orders 0870 600 5522
Fax orders 0870 600 5533

www.thestationeryoffice.com
www.schoolmanager.net

The Stationery Office Bookshops
123 Kingsway, London WC2B 6PQ
020 7242 6393 Fax 020 7242 6412
68–69 Bull Street, Birmingham B4 6AD
0121 236 9696 Fax 0121 236 9699
33 Wine Street, Bristol BS1 2BQ
0117 926 4306 Fax 0117 929 4515
9–21 Princess Street, Manchester M60 8AS
0161 834 7201 Fax 0161 833 0634
16 Arthur Street, Belfast BT1 4GD
028 9023 8451 Fax 028 9023 5401
The Stationery Office Oriel Bookshop
18–19, High Street, Cardiff CF1 2BZ
029 2039 5548 Fax 029 2038 4347
71 Lothian Road, Edinburgh EH3 9AZ
0870 606 5566 Fax 0870 606 5588

The Stationery Office's Accredited Agents
(see Yellow Pages)

and through good booksellers

Contents

Contents

Professional Excellence in Schools

The Professional Excellence in Schools programme endeavours to deliver authoritative information and professional guidance to education management teams in clear and easily accessible formats.

Professional Excellence in Schools is produced by The Stationery Office by a fully integrated team of expert education professionals and established content providers. We are dedicated to delivering the Professional Excellence in Schools programme to the highest standard which will make it a key source of information and guidance that facilitate the management of schools and the professional development of the education community.

Each series within Professional Excellence in Schools concentrates on a core management function and is designed to provide education professionals with the complete management solution.

Introduction to the series

The purpose of this series of short books is to make available readable, up-to-date views on educational issues and controversies connected with leadership and management. The principal aim is to provide texts which will support individual and collective professional learning to those new to school leadership roles, and those aspiring to take on leadership responsibilities. The series should also help serving headteachers and governors to review topics of relevance to the implementation of their roles and responsibilities.

This series attempts to provide general coverage of leadership and management issues. Its focus is upon motivating and developing people, thereby sustaining and improving the learning process and schools as a whole. The first title takes a pragmatic approach to understanding leadership and how it links with corporate decisions and corporate activities. The other books will look in more detail at human and systems aspects of leadership and how these connect with the change process. The general approach is to try to provide information of wide practical relevance, supported by problem-solving activities which engage the reader as a reflective practitioner.

The basic structure is the same across all of the books, thus providing a uniformity of approach, but the strengths and expertise of each team of authors is used to the full. The individual authors have been encouraged to give a personal interpretation of their topic and the way it is developing. To ensure consistency and relevance, the team responsible for the series has met on numerous occasions to ensure that the books draw on practical experience and actual school contexts. By this means the team has also sought to minimise the amount of overlap between titles.

The reader is presented with a variety of types of information and this is used to both stimulate and inform. The common structure in each chapter in each book includes:

◆ 'Issues in focus' sections. These expand upon the core text by examining topical issues of relevance, or they serve to provide further comments on a key issue.
◆ Notice board information. Like a school's notice boards, these short sections are there to highlight key messages succinctly or to relay important items of communication.

◆ 'Interesting facts' seek to place key issues in the context of historical, cultural or topical material.
◆ Strategic PIN downs are practical tasks. They are designed to help the reader consider how the content may be taken further, applied to a specific managerial task, or used as a professional development activity by self and/or colleagues.

The overarching aim of the series is to provide short, portable and accessible texts which go some way towards unifying the theory and practice of leadership and management.

Preface

> 'She still seems to me in her own way a person born to command,' said Luce.
> 'I wonder if anyone is born to obey,' said Isabel.
> 'That may be why people command rather badly, they have no suitable material to work on.'
>
> Ivy Compton Bennet

You can't fault leadership! Everyone believes in it and most multinational organisations demonstrate a commitment to securing it in order to survive and progress. There are many pundits espousing different fashions of leadership, and plenty of individuals or organisations who will take money from those lining up wanting to 'learn how to lead'. Politicians, national and international movements, pressure groups and the cinematograph industry have discovered a new passion from promoting the inspiration and heroics of leadership, and it is no exaggeration to say it may soon be a compulsory element in the agenda of lifelong learning.

The trouble is over-commitment to the myth of leadership. First, it is still perceived by many as the province of unique individualism. The military, scholastic, religious or technological hero-innovator who, not having feet of clay, sweeps all aside in the pursuit of innovation, philanthropic ideals or access to the 'promised land'. Second, there is the 'cult' industry of leadership – the media experts, company figureheads and nominal public leaders who can describe leadership rather better than they can demonstrate it. These paradoxes still do not dissuade us from 'awaiting' or 'seeking' the hidden specialist or soothsayer whose steadfast stance, powerful command and benevolent authoritarianism will take charge and direct us through a process of individual or organisational change.

This book does not seek to debunk the popularism of leadership, since there are effective individuals who inspire, arouse belief and commitment, and make things better. We think, however, that even in these circumstances the full effect of leadership is a mix of their iconic gifts with the dedication and talents of those who 'serve' or 'follow'. In short, the charisma which marks out the superhero or superhead may be a valuable asset in times of crisis or doubt, but longer-term improvements and sustained change depend on ethos and strategies which enable leadership to be a 'collective shared task' operating at many different levels. It is the utilisation of the 'full human factor' which we seek to explore in the chapters which follow. We set out to cover:

- ◆ the challenge of change;
- ◆ how 'leadership' as opposed to leader is conceived;
- ◆ how leadership fits in to the professional demands and structures of schools today;
- ◆ the interrelationship between leadership and management functions;
- ◆ the climate and circumstances which enable others to meet leadership challenges;
- ◆ the practice of leadership as a catalyst for creativity.

We hope the book will help define the substantive thing called 'leadership'. We also hope it will help those who have to face the day-to-day reactive challenges and the proactive opportunities that comprise life in school.

Anonymous

'Remember, we all stumble, every one of us. That's why it's a comfort to go hand-in-hand.'

1.1 Overview

The principal challenge facing everyone in education, but more especially those holding some office of leadership, is the task of dealing with new expectations, new situations, new problems, heightened uncertainty and increased ambiguity. In short, coping with consistent and accelerating change. There is now less stability in national and international structures, less ease in forecasting and planning for the future, and less familiarity in the look of social conventions, social arrangements and social relationships. It is tempting to view present-day changes as beyond the control of any individual or single organisation. The contrary view is to see change as a normal part of our lives, and as an opportunity for innovation and the creation of improvement. This chapter begins with a description of how current changes are perceived. It continues with an examination of issues which arise for schools, teachers and students. It concludes with some thoughts on educational direction.

1.2 Features of change

'Nothing is permanent except change.'

Heraclitus

As national and global demands engulf us, politicians and the public look to schools to survive the buffeting waves of present changes, while training the next generation of mariners to face uncertain seas and tempest. This requires of school captains and their crew firm-footedness on a rolling deck, the tenacity to calm and guide others who feel that change will be all storm and no respite, the steadfastness to set and maintain a good course in the height of the gale, and the optimism to expect and seek worthwhile gains beyond the existing horizon.

No leader of an education team is exempt from these expectations. They are asked to show on the bridge, at one and the same time, strong inspiration, coupled with competent navigation, seamanship and crew management. They must do all this while coping themselves with adapting to constant change as being the new elixir of modern domestic, personal and professional life.

Chapter 1

Alphonse Karr   *'The more things change, the more they stay the same.'*

Some people draw an analogy between any type of change and the fairground carousel. Watch it long enough and the same thing passes by time and time again, albeit it in slightly different guises, colours and adornments, as the years and seasons pass. Others regard change as fixed and progressive, with different and profound influences on the present arising from irreversible economic, social and technological forces. They see change not as adaptations to the fairground carousel but the replacement of the fairground by the adventure ride and theme park.

The one view suggests 'microtrends' – a continual process of change but more that of shifting emphasis than radicalism (the carousel view) – others refer to fundamental 'megatrends', that is, significant economic and social changes with long lasting and irreversible influence (the new development view). It is feasible to suggest that in education both types of change prevail at present, as indicated by Notice board 1.

Notice board 1 Micro and mega trends

Microtrends (Reshaped trends – Carousel)	Megatrends (New and permanent influences)
◆ The aims and objectives of schooling.	◆ The rise of the 'corporate influence' – national and international policies, the perspectives of the multinationals, the effects of globalisation.
◆ Differing and developing views of intelligence – e.g. multiple intelligence, including 'emotional intelligence'.	◆ The continual changing nature of employment and unemployment as new technologies and the world economy unfold.
◆ The focus of assessment and the manner and means of assessing learning outcomes.	◆ Re-examination of and challenge to 'authority' – legal, family, professional and religious.
◆ The development of initial reading and reading development skills.	◆ Very rapid growth in knowledge, particularly in science and technology.
◆ The means of managing and meeting student diversity.	◆ Privatisation and centralisation.
◆ Teaching methods.	◆ The use of cheap and integrated ICT.
◆ The nature and purposes of homework.	◆ A more mobile world population with an increasing age profile.
◆ The role of performance management and targeting.	◆ Recognising and assimilating gender and cultural distinctiveness.
◆ The aims, manner, means and resourcing of teachers' professional development.	◆ National and international unease about the growth of an 'underclass' – those with no real stake or faith in current structures and values.

> 'We constantly seem to be attempting to use yesterday's organisation today to get us to tomorrow, which won't even be there when we arrive.'

Stanley Davis

If this analysis is correct, the prevailing rate of change in the organisation and methodology of schooling is slower and less profound than the social and economic milieu it serves. The need to close this gap means that the pressure on education leaders has never been sharper or more forceful. Thus, those exercising individual and collective leadership face an ever increasing range of professional challenges. Some of these challenges are identified in Issues in focus 1.1.

Issues in focus 1.1

The impact of 'megatrends' is acknowledged in the *National Standards for Headteachers*. Items of particular relevance include:

Section 3: professional knowledge and understanding

g. political, economic, social, religious and technological influences which have an impact on strategic operational planning and delivery;

i. management, including employment law, equal opportunities legislation, personnel, external relations, finance and change;

p. strategies for teaching pupils about ethnic and cultural diversity.

Section 4: skills and attributes

Attributes:

ii. adaptability to changing circumstances and new ideas.

Section 5: key areas for headship

Strategic direction and development of the school
[D]evelop a strategic view for the school in its community and analyse and plan for its future needs and further development within the local, national and international context.

Teaching and learning

vii. create and promote positive strategies for developing good race relations and dealing with racial harassment.

It can be argued that the range and level of these challenges are already well beyond those which earlier practitioners had to surmount. The position in respect of legislated change is well described by Brighouse and Woods (1999):

'Nowadays, the hailstorm of externally mandated change is overwhelming and socially disturbing to the rhythms of successful teaching, learning and schooling. New methods of dealing with it are extensive.'

p.60

Strategic PIN down – Reflection 1.1	**Aims**
	◆ to decide what factors may shape education in the future;
	◆ to help the school to be forward-looking and proactive.

P – State the PROBLEM	Megatrends have implications for schools at the levels of policy ...
I – Clarify the ISSUE	The chief issue is balancing changing expectations and directions with ...
N – Tackle the NEED	The primary need is to establish medium and longer-term planning in a manner which is sufficiently flexible to ...

Before you begin, decide:
- ◆ what the stable or relatively enduring influences are;
- ◆ what you can't be certain about but will need to monitor;
- ◆ what firm ground you can secure in a week, next month, in six months – rather than 'sometime';
- ◆ how you can network with other schools and organisations facing similar challenges.

Tip
It may be helpful to group 'megatrends' under the headings economic, environmental, social and technological.

1.3 Changing needs

'Change comes from small initiatives which work, initiatives which when imitated, become the fashion. We cannot wait for great visions from great people, for they are in short supply at the end of history. It is up to us to light our own small fires in the darkness.'

Charles Handy

1.3.1 Schools

It is reasonable to assume that in the years and decades ahead, the school environment will become an even sharper microcosm of local, national and global influences. This means that school leadership will have to learn to live with:

◆ diffuse boundaries between schools and other organisations;
◆ less 'steady state' activities and routines;
◆ further questioning of educational values and school efficacy;
◆ regular, microscopic review of learning outcomes;
◆ more student diversity;
◆ increased flexibility in timetabling, programmes of study and study arrangements;
◆ rapidly developing technologies;
◆ new or broader professional responsibilities;
◆ tighter examination of cost-effectiveness.

The knock-on consequence of this is that schools will need to grow and be centres of continual learning. The school as an institution will have to learn alongside its staff as they seek to better match professionalism to changing local, national and international demands; alongside its parents as they seek to balance community, domestic, economic, interpersonal and social pressures, and alongside its students as they strive to meet attainment targets, while harmonising spiritual, moral, social and cultural development.

If learning is a key element for all in facing the challenges of survival and development, it follows that the school has to develop as a 'learning organisation'. It has to put into practice, at the school level, the same central objective it pursues with its students. That is, 'learning how to learn' is seen as being a more important professional accomplishment, than merely achieving a set of administrative competencies or learning more about the institution as an organisation.

> ## Issues in focus 1.2
>
> Most organisations who learn as they serve people or produce goods have identifying characteristics. These characteristics have been summarised in different ways by different writers – see, for example, Garratt (1994), Lawlor (1999) and West-Burnham and O'Sullivan (1998). In general, the chief characteristics are said to be:
>
> ◆ a climate which helps free flow and divergence to emerge;
> ◆ a perception that learning is an organic process, it is cyclical, continuous, re-shaping and never finished;
> ◆ an attitude which seeks 'best-fit' rather than 'perfect solutions'; fitting strategies or ideas to the context and the moment, but accepting the need to revise or restructure as circumstances require;
> ◆ an approach which identifies organisational tasks, for example, forecasting and forward planning, resource management and the evaluation of outcomes as potential opportunities to learn and develop;
> ◆ an environment where people are encouraged to learn for themselves and to use their learning to help solve problems;
> ◆ an acknowledgement that teachers are the principal 'experts' in learning and teaching, as well as individual learners in their own right.
>
> As with leadership itself, there is no one type or one style of 'learning organisation'. The approach developed in any one company, institution, school or service will mirror the learning process *per se*. The approach will be ongoing, showing different preferences about how to learn, undertaking appropriate reframing of the learning objectives in response to changing circumstances, and reflecting variable levels of effectiveness and success in the life cycle of the organisation. It is not just an adopted stance to 'organisational learning' but a vibrant problem-solving process which has to be sustained and promoted.

1.3.2 Teachers

If teachers are not to become merely agents of central government initiatives and reforms, they will need to spend more time and energy reflecting on what education is for and how their professional efforts and those of their school can serve the best of educational values. They will need to couple such thinking with action-research, however informally organised, which at one and the same time *proves* the quality of the school and *improves* the quality of the school. Their own professional development will need to centre less on core knowledge and specific skills, and more on understanding the learning process at the individual, group, team and organisational levels. They will have to learn more about the teacher as a leader, as well as the teacher as lead learner. Encouraging reflective practice will involve collecting evidence about pupils' learning, plus individual and group analysis of how to bring about improvement. Teachers will increasingly learn from each other and from pupils.

Barth (1990) provides a powerful comment on this issue:

> 'To assert one's leadership as a teacher, often against forces of administrative resistance, takes commitment to an educational ideal. It requires the energy to combat one's own inertia caused by habit and overwork. And it requires a certain kind of courage to step outside the small prescribed circle of traditional "teacher tasks", to declare through our actions that we care about and take responsibility for more than the minimum, more than what goes on within the four walls of our classrooms.'
>
> p.131

The relationship between students' levels of academic achievement and teachers' commitment and well-being is reasonably well researched and fairly conclusive. In general, the higher the level of personal well-being and professional respect, the better teachers commit and do, as measured by indices of attendance, burnout, classroom ethos, the quality of students' learning and achievement, and the rates of teacher turnover.

In contrast, research which attempts to examine the effects of teacher involvement in school-based self-managed teams for decision-making, strategic planning, school self-evaluation and school promotion purposes, is sparse, more recent and less secure in terms of findings. It is clear that acceptance of the school's aims and values influences commitment, and that morale is determined in large measure by the perceptions that teachers have of their value to the school and to the society, the outcomes their students achieve in academic and other accomplishments, and the freedom of action they as teachers have in supporting the school's agenda and goals.

How far teachers' morale and effectiveness are influenced by their perceptions of educational and societal changes is even less well known, but general observation and anecdotal commentary over the last decade or so suggest that they feel unduly stifled and inhibited by narrow dictates, excessive centralisation and harsh judgemental statements on performance from those 'not in the line of fire'. In terms of the psychological construct of 'locus of control', there is much yet to be done to convince teachers that balance can be achieved between internal and external influences over success and failure.

That is not to say that teachers have an innate disposition to be against change. Most will, in fact, corral and utilise major initiatives, if they perceive these to have benefits for their students and the community their school serves. Like most other professionals, however, they wilt under constant negative press and seemingly endless criticism from those whose 'ideology increases with their distance from the problem'. In contrast, like most other groups, they thrive when offered inspiration and creative challenge.

This means that if teachers are to play a full part in the response schools make to economic, social and technological challenges, it is essential that those who train them, direct them, lead them, pay them and inspect them, go beyond rhetoric and policy statements on excellence. They need to present genuine passion for the cause, based on a determination to inspire and support those who must achieve the excellence they expound. As Peters and Austin asserted as long ago as 1985, a search for excellence in the absence of a passion to support the creativity and commitment which make a difference, is like planting seeds in an arid desert. If teachers are both to be well led and in turn to lead well, though leadership training and the National College for School Leadership may help, we have to give the right level of attention to Peters and Austin's straightforward formula for difference:

> '[F]or the last twenty-five years we have carried around with us the model of manager as cop, referee, devil's advocate, dispassionate analyst, professional decision-maker, naysayer, pronouncer. The alternative we now propose is leader – as cheerleader, enthusiast, nurturer of champions, hero finder, wanderer, dramatist, coach, facilitator, builder. It's not a model of what might be, or a prescription for the impossible. We've learned it in real time, from people who've done it in the glamour industries and those who've won in extremely adverse situations ... From all these people we've learned nothing about magic. We've learned instead about passion, care, intensity, consistency, attention, drama, of the implicit and explicit use of symbols – in short, of inspired and committed leadership.'

p. xix

Thus, those external to schools and those inside, have to give teachers courage, heart, inspiration and vision, more than they give them policy statements, measurement data, achievement targets and professional standards.

Strategic PIN down – Reflection 1.2	**Aims**
	◆ to consider what the school might do to maintain teacher morale and commitment;
	◆ to examine the school's contribution to creating a collective feel-good factor.

P – State the PROBLEM	If teachers are a cornerstone of a school's success they ...
I – Clarify the ISSUE	Avoiding bland positivism, but creating a sense of ...
N – Tackle the NEED	To demonstrate individual and team worth we should ...

Before you begin, decide:

◆ what influences are involved, e.g. demonstrating a professional example; having high expectations;

◆ what information is needed, e.g. clear knowledge about teachers' work; evidence of positive achievements;

◆ what needs to be avoided, e.g. commending every action and task, regardless of value; slipping into condescension.

Tip

Think about what worthwhile representation the school can bring to terms such as applauding effort; bullet pointing gains; clarity of intent; delegation; openness; pastoral support for staff; praise; school culture, stress reduction and support.

1.3.3 Students

'Teaching children to count is not as important as teaching them what counts.'

Anonymous

Some current educational objectives can appear to be too instrumental, too short-sighted and rather banal in an age when many adults are as insecure as their adolescents, when some children are having children, when society has found the need to expand maximum security units for young offenders, when in some countries teenagers are on death row, and when some students are hooked on drugs and despair before they have completed their school years.

Certainly the up and down pressures of a changing world and the accompanying changing values are felt as much, if not more acutely by the young, than the rest of society. That many students do as well as they do in school, in youth award schemes, in voluntary service, in post-school education and in their careers and communities is a mixture of luck, their own resilience and the quality of their upbringing and education.

It is now firmly recognised that the curriculum should enable young people to understand themselves, to be aware of their responsibilities and rights, to appreciate how 'community' revolves around care, commitment and capability, to understand what responsibility as a 'citizen and parent' means, and to realise that they can be catalysts for positive change in their schools, clubs, colleges, workplaces and within local, national and international enterprises.

There is recognition too that students have to be prepared to accept that life is not static but ever changing; that they will face changes not necessarily experienced by their parents. For example:

◆ less employment security;
◆ greater ethical tensions as genetics, and medical and communications technology pose new dilemmas;
◆ a world with diminished natural power resources;
◆ the effects of global warming;
◆ increased world competition and possible escalation of conflict;
◆ growing fragmentation in the way families, communities and political institutions are structured and organised;
◆ greater and glaring dependence on new technologies.

However, they may well experience new horizons or new advantages undreamed of in previous decades, for example, even better health than now; more sharing of cultural diversity; greater choice of domestic, environmental and leisure services; new forms of travel, including possibly space travel; unprecedented ways of thinking or new innovations to help deal with moral challenges and material requirements, and possibly more beneficial political discourse.

To cope with these scenarios, students will need to be better than ever knowledge-determiners, knowledge-creators and knowledge-users. They will need to be creative and flexible thinkers. Their education will have to be truly broad, balanced and relevant, and schools will be the secure environment in which to grow academically and socially. Though literacy, numeracy and information and communication technology skills now constitute the main agenda for student development, of equal importance will be the ability to work effectively in teams, to solve problems, to make decisions and to think in innovative ways.

Issues in focus 1.3

The cyclical nature of changing local, national and international circumstances, and their implications for students' education and lives, are recognised and well described by the Government's recent Advisory Group on Citizenship (DfEE/QCA 1998). Their response is to argue for stronger representation of citizenship teaching in schools and for increased use of community-centred learning. They define 'citizenship' and outline essential concepts, values, knowledge, skills and understanding which students should acquire before the end of compulsory schooling.

Strategic PIN down – Reflection 1.3	Aims	
	◆ to examine principles for guiding citizenship teaching;	
	◆ to consider the school's current response to citizenship education;	
	P – State the PROBLEM	Schools can only do so much. What they can do is ...
	I – Clarify the ISSUE	Most guiding principles will be within the schools' general aims. Those exclusive to citizenship education are ...
	N – Tackle the NEED	Establish how far the school already provides an entitlement to citizenship education. Put in place a timetable to extend and deepen the range and quality of appropriate experiences. We will seek to achieve ... by ...
	Before you begin. reflect on:	
	◆ which whole school issues apply;	

Strategic PIN down – Reflection 1.3, cont.

◆ what messages there are for teaching approaches and learning opportunities;

◆ what the relationships are between assessment of learning and assessment for learning;

◆ what the implications for subject teaching and cross-curricular themes are.

Tip

Look at pages 44 to 61 of the Advisory Group's report on citizenship to help audit where the school is now and what it needs to do next.

Interesting facts 1 Citizenship in education

Throughout the ages, education for citizenship has been variably promoted for some or all members of society. In the European sphere, such promotion has included attention to the two main aspects of citizenship – first, the status of 'citizen' with its accompanying rights and duties; and second, a person's day-to-day 'conduct' as a citizen.

◆ Greek sophists declare themselves to be 'professors of moral improvement'.

◆ Greek culture emphasises that young men should 'learn the laws' and live according to the pattern they provide.

◆ Plato and Aristotle present justice as essentially a 'social virtue'.

◆ Plato's *Republic* outlines three classes of citizen. The improvement of the 'soul and character' are seen as significant educational goals. In the *Laws* Plato calls for co-education and for serious consideration on how best to educate the 'citizen-ruler'.

◆ The Roman orator Quintilian describes the 'perfect man' and the training needed to produce such a person.

◆ Religious orders are active in the development of learning and the beginnings of the universities. More's *Utopia* and Elgot's *Governour* re-examine the principles of morality as the regulator of conduct.

◆ Ignatius Loyola founds the Jesuit system to 'arrest' disintegrating forces on religious life and moral education.

◆ Comenius advocates the 'common school' with training for all in 'modesty, sociability and politeness'. In *The Great Didactic* he calls for near universal education and the inclusion of girls – '*They are endowed with equal sharpness of mind and the capacity for knowledge, and they are able to attain the highest positions, since they have often been called by God Himself to rule over nations. Why, therefore, should we admit them to the alphabet and afterwards drive them away from books?'*

◆ Milton develops the 'civic function' of education and includes (as Plato and others did) the 'care of the body'. The place of health education within the school's curriculum begins to take shape.

◆ Locke appeals for direct lessons about, and practice of, values. *'Tis virtue then, direct virtue which is the hard and valuable part to be aimed at in education .... all other considerations and accomplishments should give way and be postponed to this'.*

◆ Rousseau sees adolescent development as a critical period of preparation for playing a part in the moral and social order. The adolescent must study himself in relation to his fellow-man and the 'ways of the world'.

◆ Froebel indicates that 'all round development' is the principal aim of education and childhood is the 'most important stage in the total development of man and humanity'.

◆ Spencer classifies activities in their order of importance for human life – biological, social, political and cultural.

◆ Kant stresses 'good will' as the most important moral quality of the person – the capacity to act according to one's sense of 'duty' rather than merely on the current feelings or tendencies which influence one.

◆ Ruskin declares, *'There is no wealth but life.'* Puts forward practical schemes for social education.

◆ Dewey promotes 'life itself' as the ground experience for the education of the child.

◆ Piaget and Kohlberg set out important features and stages affecting cognitive and moral development.

◆ 1960–80. Significant exploration of the contribution of personal and social education to the development of moral, well-balanced citizens. Important milestones include DES/HMI publications on the curriculum; the development by the Schools Council of project materials in the areas of civic, social and moral education; the establishment of the Assessment of Performance Unit (1974) and its decision to include 'personal and social education' as one of seven priorities for the curriculum; and the Further Education Unit's (1980) attention to social competencies and 'social and life skills'.

◆ 1989 National Curriculum Council's (NCC) Circular No. 6 – Education for citizenship. This is now one of five cross-curricular themes.

◆ November 1990 – NCC issues Curriculum Guidance 8 – Education for Citizenship.

◆ 1997 Concerns that Citizenship as a subject is diminishing in importance and impact. Government resolves 'to strengthen education for citizenship and the teaching of democracy in schools' (White Paper, *Excellence in Schools* – November 1997).

◆ Advisory Group on Citizenship established. Issues final report in September 1988.

◆ National Curriculum Key Stages 3 and 4, programmes of study for citizenship – statutory from August 2002.

1.4 Educational direction

Anonymous   *'Past experience should be a guidepost – not a hitching post.'*

Assessing what has been said so far leads to the conclusion that more than ever schools need to muster clarity about their beliefs and what 'educational direction' means specifically for them. Professional leadership includes creating a vision and establishing the clearest direction possible. But this challenge is not a solitary activity for the head. It involves listening to staff, agreeing with the school community a picture for the future, and involving staff in charting this vision and planning the route towards it.

This aspect of leadership will need to operate at all levels of practice – school, team and classroom. Leaders at these levels have, therefore, to constantly examine their own values, beliefs, attitudes and behaviour; relate these to those held by their colleagues, and agree the best collective perspective and corporate approach. Such constant 'self-evaluation' provides an individual and team 'reference system' against which to check progress towards meeting the school's broader vision, the requirements laid down in national goals, and the objectives outlined in the school's policy statements.

Creating the overall vision and extracting from it a priority agenda of next steps direction has to be co-terminous with creating a school culture of openness, trust, teamwork and collegiality, since it is only within such a culture that genuine shared vision and direction can be shaped. This issue is explored further in the chapters which follow. Suffice it here to say that in order to create a firm vision and direction for the school, values will have to be made explicit, explored and eventually framed in a manner which allows all stakeholders to relate to them. It is essential not to make the vision so esoteric that it cannot be translated easily into day-to-day practice. It is also important to ensure that the vision balances between holding on to that which is good, setting aspirations for the future, and determining next stage changes and improvements.

It follows that leaders must have the confidence to communicate this picture in a meaningful and reassuring way, including linking the school's good practice with any proposed new strategies for responding effectively to internal and external demands. Such confidence results from regularly applying the skills of constructive listening, empathising, negotiating, networking and showing fair resolve in the face of challenges and conflict. It is also founded on knowing that the broad parameters of the vision are grounded in short- and medium-term priorities, and, in turn, these are expressed in educational objectives and learning outcomes which are understood by all the members of the school community. A strong link between the more distant horizon and the actualities of day-to-day planning is usually forged by following some development/review paradigm, for example, the use of the acronym SMARTER planning. That is:

> **S**pecific outcomes.
> **M**easurable – and with clear success criteria.
> **A**greed – by all key players.
> **R**ealistic – in terms of immediate capabilities and resources.
> **T**ime-marked, within an immediate, short- and longer-term calendar scale.
> **E**valuated – by reference to actual outcomes and the broad agenda of planned changes.
> **R**eviewed – as part of a cyclical sequence of planning and development.

Clearly, the paradigm in itself is only a professional tool. It is the staff's overall commitment, creativity, resolve and their reflective capabilities that will turn the acronym into a rich and corporate school development plan.

Strategic PIN down – Reflection 1.4	**Aim**
	◆ to explore the issues of (i) a personal reference system; (ii) good listening; and (iii) success criteria.

P – State the PROBLEM	Vision and direction need to be clear and accessible. This implies ...
I – Clarify the ISSUE	The vision and expected outcomes need to be understood by all stakeholders. To ensure this ...
N – Tackle the NEED	The vision must galvanise and motivate others, therefore ...

A Constructing a personal reference system

List the five most important and/or influential values and beliefs for you as a leader.

PERSONAL REFERENCE SYSTEM

1
2
3
4
5

B Being a good listener

Devise your own checklist of items that will help you develop good listening skills.

BEING A GOOD LISTENER

1
2
3
4
5
6

Discuss these with a colleague and see if any crucial items are missing.

C Evaluating for improvement

Choose one of the planned outcomes from the school's vision/mission statement (or from an area of work for which you are responsible) and list five criteria that will show the outcome has been successful.

Strategic PIN down – Reflection 1.4 cont.

PLANNED OUTCOMES: SUCCESS CRITERIA

Intended outcome:

_____

How has this been made clear to all stakeholders?

Success criteria

1

2

3

4

5

Share the criteria with a colleague or team. Add to the list – or modify it after this consultation.

1.5 Summary

> 'One cannot step in the same river twice.'

Heraclitus

◆ Change is ever present and always will be.

◆ Change is both recycled themes with new colours and fundamental, irreversible difference.

◆ The expectation of a suitable professional response to the demands of change will increase, not decrease.

◆ Schools cannot control economic, social and technological changes, but they can anticipate some trends, seek to be proactive rather than just reactive, and look to develop strategies which help staff and students cope with changing circumstances.

◆ Though mandated change has to be complied with, schools can and should have their own development identity.

◆ To respond effectively to mandated and self-chosen change, the school itself has to engage in the learning process. It has to become a true 'learning organisation'.

◆ Knowing 'how' and 'why' is more important than knowing 'what'.

◆ Balancing the demands of external changes and pressures with internal school aspirations, conditions and dynamics is essential.

◆ Coping requires attention to human as well as organisational needs.

◆ Self-reflection on values, beliefs, attitudes and patterns of professional behaviour is an essential characteristic of good leadership.

◆ Educational vision and direction need to be clear, accessible, understood by all stakeholders and framed in a manner which allows for practical review and evaluation.

2.1   Overview

In this chapter we examine some of the different perspectives on 'leadership'. First, we acknowledge that the term has many shades of meaning and attracts various academic and professional interpretations. Next, we consider leadership as a form of career goal or the delivery of a specific type of organisational role. Finally, we look at the popular image of leadership and its expression as a set of personal attributes. We offer this overview for two important reasons. First, in recognition that the manner of carrying out a function is largely determined by our experience of it as portrayed by others, coupled with our existing thinking of how it should be done. Second, because we believe it follows from this premise, that knowing more about the concept of leadership, how it is described and how it is practised, should help senior managers to get the best from themselves and from their teams, thereby enhancing the quality of education their school provides.

2.2   Perspectives on leadership

> 'And seek for truth in the groves of Academe.'

Horace

There are many different perspectives on leadership. They are drawn from a variety of academic disciplines and from various professional contexts. Notice board 2 illustrates some of the diversity.

Notice board 2 Key disciplines/key stakeholders with an interest in leadership	
Key disciplines	**Key stakeholders**
◆ Business science	◆ Business managers
◆ Education theory	◆ Chief executives
◆ History	◆ Directors
◆ Military science	◆ Educationalists
◆ Political science	◆ Media representatives
◆ Psychology	◆ Military strategists
◆ Sociology	◆ Politicians
	◆ Social scientists

Despite the number of research studies and other means of investigating leadership – estimated in education alone to be over 10,000 in 1991 (Walker, 1994, quoted in Thody, 1997) – no one discipline or perspective can yet claim to have established accuracy in definition or description. The present state of play is a profusion of influences, concepts and terminology. To date, cross-reference is limited and there are academic and professional barriers to the fluid cross-fertilisation of ideas. What is certain is that leadership is not an abstract concept. It only has meaning and purpose within defined contexts, situations or role relationships. Effectiveness in one context, situation or role, will not guarantee success in another.

2.3 Leadership as uniqueness or leadership in all

Shakespeare

'Some are born great, some achieve greatness and some have greatness thrust upon them.'

Everyday life shows us people who have a certain 'natural presence' – even if this is difficult to define. They seem 'born to lead' and can marshal personal qualities and professional skills much more easily and quickly than others.

Equally, we can see many effective headteachers, senior managers and team leaders who seemingly possess no 'special charisma', yet who achieve a balance between affiliation and authority, and who attract sufficient loyalty and commitment to get difficult work done.

Thus, leading people to be successful may result from the skilled use of a range and combination of personal characteristics, or it may arise from the consistent application of a set of honed management skills. In this sense, leadership can mean both a 'personalistic style' of approach – possibly resulting from innate human qualities – and a 'formalistic style', whereby an administrative and management culture is set in place that people appear to trust and be guided by.

The provision of effective leadership by either of these means is not necessarily the exclusive reserve of one individual. The effectiveness may result from a pervasive process in which team energy and collective skills gel into a harmonious strategy that goes beyond the charisma and competence of any one individual. Warren Bennis, an American writer on leadership, believes that more collaborative forms of leadership result largely from the emergence of intellectual capital as the most important element in organisational success. He thinks that leadership is about unleashing the genius of colleagues within a clear vision and direction and in a climate of trust and success (Sammon, paper presented at orientation Brathay Conference, 1998). Therefore a pervasive energy may develop and collect its own infectious force, particularly where many people become motivated to succeed 'for the team' and then progressively learn to do important things in effective ways.

Issues in focus 2.1

Across the academic-professional continuum this dichotomy is captured in an ongoing and rigorous debate about how far leadership should be conceived as the influence of 'greatness', and the application of 'qualities' beyond those which most people have, versus whether a conception of leadership as the reserve of those with 'invigorating uniqueness' is misleading and professionally restrictive.

In education, this debate centres on what weight should be given to the headteacher as 'top dog' – acting as the chief provider of vision, energy and commitment to the staff and students, who then serve in a kind of 'dependent' mode – contrasted with the notion that leadership effectiveness is a talent that should be nurtured in everyone and throughout all the teams and social units of the school. Too much publicity for the notion of success emanating principally from an individual 'hero-innovator' runs the risk of deskilling others, and possibly leaving them to adopt a position whereby they abdicate any responsibility for the quality of the school as a whole. On the other hand, too little attention to delegating responsibilities for distinct aspects of administration and management to key figures may result in a *laissez-faire* situation in which an institution becomes rudderless and adrift without adequate navigation. The reader will find that Gronn (1999) provides interesting comment on these different perceptions of leadership. He concludes:

> '[W]e all lead, for at least some of the time, or we are led, for pretty well all of the time. Some of us want to be leaders. Others are content to be followers. We make choices, or at least we think we do. How and why it is that particular choices in respect of leading and following come to be made throughout our lives, and what the parameters and confines are within which those choices are made, are part and parcel of leadership careers.'

p. 20

21

Strategic PIN down – Reflection 2.1	**Aims**
	◆ to reflect on the essential qualities and skills of individual and collective leadership;
	◆ to begin to decide what a professional framework for the development of leadership might look like.

P – State the PROBLEM	Effective leadership results from an amalgam of ....
I – Clarify the ISSUE	It develops out of a mixture of ...
N – Tackle the NEED	A professional leadership framework will include ...

Before you begin:

◆ consider and prepare, or team brainstorm and prepare, a list of 40 positive statements relating to the perception and practice of leadership (for example, 'leadership is co-ordinated team endeavour'; 'leadership is the confidence to inspire others', etc.);

◆ after the list has been generated, draw up a grid.

Table 2.1

L	
E	
A	
D	
E	
R	
S	
H	
I	
P	

Now, using the list and any points from the reflection or brainstorming session, complete the grid by using each letter to exemplify this statement: Leadership means to ...

Finally, consider what implications the grid has for a professional framework to develop leadership.

Tip

Think about what needs to be represented in the framework, e.g. the functions of leadership; an operational definition of leadership; a description of what good leadership looks like; some indication of the practical skills needed for individual and collective leadership, and so on.

2.4 Leadership through career progression

'Go the extra mile. It's never crowded.'

Anonymous

There is much investment in commercial, educational, military and social institutions in developing the concept of leadership as career progression. The 'career profile', which steers individuals towards taking on increased responsibilities to lead others, is so well enshrined in modern employment culture, that the pressure to both *act* to take on such responsibility and to successfully *react* to it once it is acquired is considerable.

There are also other common features when one views leadership from a career standpoint. First, is the element of *ambition*. Few people achieve leadership of organisations like public services, or institutions like schools, without aspiring to *be there*. The career structure is such that this is not an arena where many, if any, have 'greatness thrust upon them' – though some who don't naturally aspire may be coerced or nudged.

The normal route is traditionally set. It is to aspire to the top post after 'serving time' in those career steps usually regarded as the necessary building blocks. These responsibilities are normally served in contexts regarded as 'familiar and similar', that is within schools or closely related educational services – a type of leadership apprenticeship within the 'family firm'. There have been attempts to break this grip, for example, Coventry LEA as early as 1973 appointed as a principal to one of their community colleges, an educational professional whose experience was naval, rather than within the norms of school progression but such radicalism has seldom been repeated, though in recent times the boundary line between serving in public service management and serving in a management capacity in the private sector has become more permeable.

The second element is *selection*. This may be by informal self-review of one's readiness to take on a particular leadership role, or more commonly, by passing through the conventional routes of a supported application, scrutiny of one's CV, short-list, interview and appointment. The interview process may or may not be supplemented by the inclusion of task-related activities, or the use of a formal 'assessment centre', and the timescale from the start of selection to finish may be very brief or more drawn out. Reliability and validity of all these forms of selection can be variable.

More recently, within educational provision, the armed services and the police, strategies have been put into place to pick up the 'aspirant' leader and guide and support them by providing a preparatory course of training before they reach the selection and appointment stage. With regard to the schooling sector, Ministers intend that such a preparatory stage should be mandatory by 2002. Thus, all those coming new to headship will have the National Professional Qualification for Headship (NPQH). This qualification is based on:

> *'national standards that set out the key knowledge, understanding, skills and attributes for the key tasks of headship. The NPQH is part of the Government's drive to develop schools that are better in every way.'*

DfEE, 1999

This takes us to the third common element of career leadership. This is *defined professionalism* – the knowledge, understanding, skills and attributes which serve as a rite of passage up the career ladder.

In one form or another, guidelines or criteria have always been around, even if they have been implicit rather than explicit. The present trend, however, is to articulate them as clearly as possible, and to make them publicly explicit in the form of schedules of professional standards, profiles of competencies, or dimensions of essential characteristics. Each of these models of school leadership has a different rationale. Equally, the range of professional areas covered, the type of criteria used, and the headings for organising them, vary somewhat from scheme to scheme.

Issues in focus 2.2

While many people agree that there is value in being more explicit about the characteristics of skilled professionalism, the best means of doing this is not without controversy. There are various models around to link qualified teacher status and the performance of practising teachers, including headteachers, to the achievement of and fluent use of certain professional capabilities. Competence-based approaches to teacher-education were prevalent in the USA in the 1970s and began to influence professional training in the UK through the competence-based vocational qualifications developed during the 1980s. Later, significant aspects of competence-based performance began to influence initial and continuing professional development for teachers (McLelland, 1973). Such developments have stalled somewhat on the divisions between competence $\downarrow$

defined as the ability to perform certain narrow professional tasks satisfactorily, and competence more broadly defined, to embrace person-related characteristics, including intellectual skills and appropriate attitudes. To some extent the 'standards' movement developed out of the competence debate. It was an attempt to define an acceptable, role-related short list of generic professional capabilities, without recourse to an endless list of numerous discrete behaviours which falsely or only crudely represent the complex whole. Both approaches are still in a state of flux. For example, there is no agreement on definitions, the balance between process and outcome indicators, the point of focus (for example, current work-based performance versus criteria indicative of future capability) and whether or not the competencies and standards should be framed in ways which make the assessment of 'levels of performance' possible.

The development of these two types of indicators grew more from the routes of seeking practical answers to the type of evidence to be presented to justify academic and professional awards, than from a solid body of research evidence. Inevitably, therefore, the emphasis has been on acquiring a framework or schedule of characteristics with good 'face validity' – that is, they look right and attract credibility with the people who demonstrate them in everyday situations. More recently, however, attention has shifted to inspection evidence and more formalised research methodology, whereby the microscope is focused sharply on what professional characteristics appear to be apparent in people who effect change. See, for example, Hay McBer (2000) and Lawlor and Sills (1999).

Strategic PIN down – Reflection 2.2	Aims
	◆ to consider the terms used to describe 'professionalism in action';
	◆ to decide which aspects of professionalism need to be described as specific and observable behaviours;
	◆ to relate this thinking to performance management.

P – State the PROBLEM	Words like attitudes, characteristics, competencies, standards and traits are ...
I – Clarify the ISSUE	Being clear on the differences between 'inference' and 'observation' requires ...
N – Tackle the NEED	Practical guidance on 'effectiveness' must ....

Before you begin, decide:

◆ some basic definitions (see the tip below);

Strategic PIN down – Reflection 2.2 cont.

◆ in what areas of 'professionalism in action' is it necessary to have a consistent approach to making judgements;

◆ what may be the consequences of loose approaches to judging 'effective professional behaviour'?

◆ what aspects of professionalism will need to be rigorously evidenced to meet the requirements of 'performance management'?

Tip

Think about how you might describe professional standards in a way which gives practical guidance, yet avoids ambiguity, narrowness and vagueness. The following summaries may help.

2.4.1 Capability

Capability is the application of ability to some desired and worthwhile end. The marshalling of knowledge, hard work, inclination, skills and temperament to get something done. Ability is 'potential' until it has been demonstrated in actual success of some kind. To be capable, one has already shown oneself to be sufficiently adept, deft, expert or proficient to secure a desired goal.

2.4.2 Characteristic

A term relating to human endeavour, it has a history in: (a) inference about human motives and behaviour – *'Let me have men about me that are fat; Sleek-headed men and such as sleep o' nights; Yond Cassius has a lean and hungry look; He thinks too much: such men are dangerous' (Julius Caesar, 1, ii, 191)*; (b) the psychology of personality, where attempts have been made to describe and explain individual differences. Such work includes trying to determine the attitudes, thinking and behaviour which makes an individual's success in one role more likely than in another, e.g. undercover agent versus general military function; aircrew rather then ground crew, etc. Seeking to distinguish the general or job-related characteristics which underpin successful human performance led to the 'holistic approach' to the assessment of personality. Its modern equivalent is the inclusion of an 'assessment centre' in the selection process. With the development of 'factor analysis' as an investigative tool, the analysis of 'key performance characteristics' for selection and training purposes has expanded rapidly across the whole area of human resource management.

2.4.3 Competence

Competence is simply the capability to 'perform a task satisfactorily' when the task is clearly defined and the 'level of performance' or the 'success to be achieved' is established; or the term can mean 'rounded professionalism' leading to the achievement of performance within the broader context of maintaining professional standards, achieving worthwhile goals, sustaining a positive disposition to others, and by reflection on individual and institutional needs securing positive responses from colleagues. The application of competence can focus on person-related or task-related ends, or both simultaneously. The term competencies is increasingly used interchangeably with characteristics. In short, competence means behaving in ways shown to be associated with successful outcomes.

2.4.4 Standards

Standards are not pure or absolute measures. The term is relative when applied to levels of academic achievement, to sport or musical prowess, to professional capabilities and to learners' competencies. Standards are set in the values and circumstances of a specific time, and the general reaction to their achievement is to raise them, thereby motivating still further improvement. Equally, comparative standards across countries and cultures are not yet on a solid base. There are often influences on learning which can account for huge differences in standards achieved by one group over another (e.g. one nation's children do far more time in school than those groups with whom they are compared). In general, it is best to regard standards as statistical indicators or sets of descriptive criteria to help shape judgements about a level of performance or the quality of a performance. They may arise from the collective opinion of 'experts' on what should be achieved by pupils of a certain age, or before the receipt of a particular academic award, or to mark reaching a stage point in a graded proficiency system. They may have some base in standardised tests results over time, or be 'best fit' descriptors of what the 'performance in action' should look like. Standards can be as capacious or as limited as those who decide them think they should be. In general, the shifting meaning of 'standards' has an intriguing history.

Interesting facts 2 Standards over time

◆ Initial link was to 'honour' and 'valour'. Demonstrated by rallying to the standard or taking 'stand' at the Royal flag or lead mast: 1138 – Battle of the Standard, Northallerton, Yorkshire.

- Came to mean 'consistency' – this being established and guaranteed by the Royal Seal. For example, the fixing of an acre and the definition of a yard by Edward 1.
- Developed with 'trade' to mean a 'common measure'. Retained link with honour – in that, by guaranteeing an open, common measure, honesty was encouraged and cheating was outlawed.
- In the 15th century, took on the meaning of 'common agreement' or general acceptance. For example, the hallmark stamped on articles of gold and silver by the assay offices as proof of recognised authenticity – hence the saying 'up to the mark'.
- By *circa* 17th or 18th centuries word had become attached to 'status' – especially standards of wealth or distinction.
- In 1876 became the 'simple school standard', i.e. a measure of performance on some task such as reciting the 7 times table. Lost link with honour and became the instrumental meaning attached to 'payment by results'. Had some tragic consequences, for example, teacher Frank Silverlock's suicide at Highbury station in 1888. Crime – some boys had shown indiscipline in class by asking questions during a parchment lesson; teacher's renewal of certificate was deferred. Silverlock wrote to parents: ' I hope my act will be forgiven, and I shall go to where there are no dull stupid boys, and no inspectors.'
- With the growth of manufacturing 'standard' became the 'product standard'.
- With the development of the concept of 'society' it became a 'marker' to help hold communities together and to give impetus to working for the common good: legal standards, social standards, a decent standard of living, etc. Later, 'standards in public life' to counteract 'sleaze' and the misuse of public office.
- Over the last 10 to 20 years, the word has become a kind of 'conceptual tool' to represent 'capability' or 'excellence' in performance: athletic, craft and musical standards, standards of scholarship. In so doing, it is returning, to some extent, to its original meaning – the effort, qualities or valour that underpin worthwhile human achievement.

The essential thing this brief history teaches us, is that achieving or defending a standard is more an intrinsic than extrinsic matter. To live up to a standard that 'I am set on believing' is important implies:

- standards succeed by 'conviction' not by simple declaration, mere explicit reference, imposition and monitoring;

- a 'performance standard' indicates the 'quality' of that which is sought and the performer understands what the quality is and 'feels like';
- the performer has the commitment to secure and sustain the standard;
- the standard is accepted as a 'range of capable performance' rather than an absolute or 'gold standard' that is always met;
- the performer believes in promoting the standard(s), not for self-aggrandisement, but to keep alive attributes and qualities thought to serve and better humankind.

2.5 The popular image of leadership

'Common sense is the ability to detect values.'

Anonymous

Real leadership is often a subtle mixture of successful action, the aura surrounding it, and the image created from it. Leadership in this sense is both perception and function. Since public perception is a powerful tool for image creation, how people describe leadership is an important influence on who leads and the manner in which they do it. This important influence reminds us that leadership has to be considered in the time and type of society in which it operates.

Notice board 3 How some people have described leadership

'He has a look upon his face that I would fain call master.'
'What is that?'
'Authority.'

Shakespeare

'As a national figure, de Gaulle attracted a fiercely loyal cadre of supporters, but he remained aloof from them, reflecting his own dictum that a leader can have "no authority without prestige, nor prestige unless he keeps his distance".' Richard Nixon

'To do great things is difficult, but to command great things is more difficult.' Friedrich Nietzsche

'My six-word formula for success with leadership – think things through, then follow through.'

Anonymous

'A new foreman joined a works where prestige had long depended on skills with the cold chisel, although this tool had actually been displaced by power machinery. The new hand aroused considerable dislike as an individual, but the men reserved their verdict on him until a break in the work, when they gathered to watch the new hand demonstrate his skill with the traditional tool. He did this very successfully and ever after retained respect as a man who "certainly knows his cold chisel".' T. Whitefield

'Example is the school of mankind, and they will learn at no other.' Burke

'Leaders of men – image fades, character lasts!' Sign on a church notice board

---

> **Notice board 3 How some people have described leadership (cont.)**
>
> *'I lead by example and persuasion and a hell of a lot of hard work. Not on the basis of power or authority. My skills are to help a large number of people to release their energies and focus themselves. It is switching on a lot of people and helping them achieve a common aim. People only do things they are convinced about. One has to create conditions in which people want to give of their best.'*
>
> *'Anyone can hold the helm when the sea is calm.'*
>
> *'A good leader inspires men to have confidence in him; a great leader inspires them to have confidence in themselves.'*
>
> These literary and popular perspectives provide important clues towards describing the effective performance people regard as 'leadership'. There are aspects of emotion and spirit involved, as well as attention to detail and structured decision-making. There are internal, intuitive characteristics, coupled with external features, such as elements of rationality. Applied intelligence and the use of appropriate or valued skills are other important elements.
>
> The best leaders probably possess a mixture of these qualities and others. There is now also increased recognition that substance is required of a leader, more than image. The constituent elements of this substance include some of the following features of effectiveness.

Sir John Harvey Jones

Publius Syrus

Anonymous

2.5.1 Being people conscious

Being a good listener, a competent observer of people. Understanding their motives and responses, and showing empathy when necessary. Displaying empathy implies being able to 'take the role of the other' and through that perception helping colleagues to marshal their assets to surmount professional challenges and problems. Being people conscious also means 'knowing the people well enough' to use their expertise and personal strengths effectively, and with this knowledge deciding how best to influence, persuade, and re-direct when such action is called for. In general, it is necessary to risk intuitive and perceptual impressions of people's habitual responses, and by doing so to become more skilled at 'reading people'.

2.5.2 Being an effective communicator

Good listening is a prerequisite for effective speaking, whether to small or large groups. Leaders have to speak with clarity and conviction and be confident of getting any message or information across to others in the team. Effective communication will involve writing clearly, accurately and concisely for a variety of audiences. Increasingly leaders require well-developed information and communication technology skills.

2.5.3 Being an effective decision-maker

This requires more than firmness and knowing the techniques and systems which aid efficient decision-making, Essentially, the capable decision-maker knows:

◆ *their own predisposition when making decisions* (for example, rash approach, gut-level response, proactive rather than reactive, analytical, calm, considered reactions which take into account the facts and options, a tendency to vacillate, and so on). This self-knowledge can be used to organise compensation (for example, more consultation and consensus seeking to balance for a personal style which is too impulsive and too risk prone) or to put in place a formal structure if one tends to be too indecisive (perhaps a published sequence and time line to highlight stages in the intended decision-making cycle);

◆ what level of *decentralisation* is possible in their school or service, such that an appropriate amount of decision-making is delegated direct to departments or teams. This distributes the power of decision-making away from one person's domination and brings it closer to the day-to-day level of actions and routines.

2.5.4 Being conscious of circumstances

This is a type of 'fitness for purpose' knowledge. It is being aware of what leadership style, what decision-making methods, and what human attributes are needed at this stage in the life of the school, service or team. The leader, along with the messages and strategies they present, must not be old-fashioned, nor so far futuristic that no rapport or credibility emerges between them and the others in the team. It is a wise leader who makes the first priority the business of deciding the priorities and who carries out the necessary level of consultation and 'taking stock' to enable any new strategy to be based on a justified mission.

2.5.5 Being value-rooted

This means believing sincerely in any new goals or standards which are to be put in place; showing by example the kind of integrity, commitment and open-mindedness which the leader expects others to follow, and demonstrating sufficient drive, energy and determination so that no one can suggest a lack of firmness about purpose. Increasingly, this is a difficult root to plant and sustain in education. This is because the political agendas of the last two decades have thrust 'window-dressing' values on schools and there has been over-direction by polemic, rather than by winning the hearts of heads and teachers to secure a mission for education which they have helped to build. Perhaps the best we can hope for here is to accept the ancient philosophical point that adversity has the effect of releasing talents which in different or less challenging circumstances may lie dormant.

2.5.6 Being an honest appraiser of self and progress

Whatever is being striven for must be kept in clear focus. The leadership must critically examine clarity and balance in targets, team deployment, team facilitation and outcomes. Effective performance means guarding against 'selectivity', that is seeing or hearing what 'one hopes is happening'. It means a ruthless determination to see the facts as they are, and hence not being blinkered by distorted perceptions of success or failure. It means supporting insights with formal data analysis.

2.5.7 Being ethical

This is not a separate moral stance the leadership takes, nor an ethical standard which is different from the general work the leadership does. It is about fairness to pupils, parents and colleagues through the quality of the service offered and the standards of education delivered. It is about being fair and consistent to individuals and groups when setting workloads, distributing resources and appraising performance. It is about fair treatment of all, and the balancing of self-interests with the needs of others.

2.5.8 Being a team builder and sustainer

Most organisations rely on teams and teamwork to achieve their goals and objectives. Since the effectiveness of any leader is only as strong as they are seen to be by those who are led, leaders need strong motivation, clear vision and direction, and team-building skills if they are to motivate and galvanise colleagues. Sustaining and developing a team require recognition and understanding of each member's strengths, weaknesses, idiosyncrasies and needs. The continuing professional development and intellectual renewal of each member of the team will be an important factor in achieving objectives.

Overall, then, popular literature and common debate confirm leadership as more than the image and status of the position held. Effective leadership emerges as a complex set of personal attributes. It requires adaptability, commitment, energy, enthusiasm, integrity, presence, perseverance, reliability and self-confidence. It is multi-faceted in terms of skills and style.

Issues in focus 2.3

An important aspect of professional capability is knowing which leadership style to adopt according to the specific context or situation. To be effective, leaders require a knowledge and understanding of the full range of leadership styles.

Authoritative

◆ leader gives orders and has a strong control instinct;
◆ characterised by high confidence and certainty of actions.

Coercive

◆ leader has a clear personal direction and vision and convinces/ persuades others to follow;
◆ following by persuasion and not orders.

Affiliative

◆ leader is always seeking harmony, establishes positive relationships and avoids conflict or confrontation;
◆ emphasis on effective communication and reliance on capabilities of staff.

Democratic

◆ leader focuses on building commitment and reaching decision by consensus and through consultation;
◆ emphasis on effective communication and reliance and capabilities of staff.

Pacesetting

◆ leader sets standards through examples;
◆ emphasis on others following the examples set;
◆ task-driven approach, with little real delegation (but overworked leader).

Coaching

◆ leader develops others through regular audit of strengths and weaknesses;
◆ emphasis on using and developing all talents in a team;
◆ leader believes in school as a learning organisation.

Headings from McBer, cited in Boyatzis, 1982

Tannenbaum and Schmidt's model of leadership styles and decision-making (1973) is similar, but uses four categories: *telling* (leader gives instruction and has a strong control instinct); *selling* (leader has clear views and values and attempts to convince others to follow); *consulting* (leader presents ideas, invites comments and suggestions, and reaches decisions by consensus); and *sharing* (leader develops other staff and delegates actions and decisions within defined limits).

Although each leader may prefer a particular style or range of styles; effective leaders utilise as broad a repertoire of styles as possible. They demonstrate the skills, knowledge and understanding to use the most appropriate style according to the specific situation or context. Different contexts may require different leadership styles, as well as different combinations of characteristics, and it is the judgement about what is appropriate that may determine effectiveness. This means that certain school situations and contexts require particular leaders. A leader who can 'shake up' an underperforming school may not always be able to maintain the resultant changes – a different type of leader may be needed to build on and sustain such changes. It is also true that some highly effective headteachers are fully aware of their strengths and dominant style and deliberately utilise the expertise and style of others in the school according to the specific situation or incident. It is worth noting that research in the USA (Rosener, 1990; Bass and Avolio, 1994) and in the UK (Macbeath, 1998; Alimo-Metcalfe, 1995; Evetts, 1994) showed clear differences in the preferred leadership styles of female and male leaders (with the Macbeath and Evetts studies looking specifically at headteachers). Female leaders were perceived generally as more democratic and less coercive than male leaders. Such research findings would appear to reinforce the need for all leaders to undertake regular reviews of their leadership styles, with a view to widening the repertoire, therefore being able to relate style more specifically to a given situation.

Strategic PIN down – Reflection 2.3	**Aims**	
	◆ to evaluate the possible advantages and disadvantages of the four styles of leadership:	
	telling (or directing)	Here is my decision. This is how we will proceed. This is what you have to do. Do this!
	selling (or coercing)	This is my thinking so far – let me convince you that it's the best way forward. This is the best option – I'll show you how it's going to meet our needs.

| **Strategic PIN down – Reflection 2.3 cont.** | consultation (discussion and collaboration) | I've prepared this picture of the situation, the challenges, the opportunities, the constraints. Let's get together and talk through possible courses of action. I'm asking each of you individually, and then collectively, what do you think we should do? |
| | delegation | The responsibility is yours. The trust is with you to make the appropriate decisions and get the job done. Please take the lead on this – I'll base the next stage of action on the advice you give. |

◆ to consider when these styles are most and least applicable.

Discuss your perceptions with colleagues. Following this, redraw Table 2.2 in a larger scale and then complete it.

Table 2.2

Style	Advantage	Disadvantage	School situation – most applicable	School situation – least applicable
Telling				
Selling				
Consultation				
Delegation				

◆ to decide which styles may need enhancement.

Take a few minutes to decide which styles need maintenance, or enhancement, by inserting one of the descriptors from the key below in every cell in Table 2.3.

Key: M = Maintenance; EH = Enhancement from in-house strategies; EE = Enhancement via external support

Table 2.3

Leadership team	Tell	Sell	Consult	Delegate
Senior management team (SMT)				
Middle managers – e.g heads of department;				
Key Stage co-ordinators SENCOs				
Teachers as classroom managers and leaders of pedagogy				
Students with responsibilities for others – e.g. members of the School Council, mentors; prefects				

Strategic PIN down – Reflection 2.3 cont.	P – State the PROBLEM	Leadership styles arise from the focus of interpretation. For a school, the most appropriate form of analysis is ....
	I – Clarify the ISSUE	Table 2.3 indicates there are many different types of leadership teams in one school community. To avoid conflict between leadership styles and their effects on the school's values, mission and development plan we need to ...
	N – Tackle the NEED	If we discover defective 'style types' we will ...

Tip

Recognise that leadership styles are cameos of how people encourage, direct and motivate real-life work situations. Know what your personal and your school's preferred or predominant style is and, if necessary, look for ways to develop greater flexibility.

2.6   Summary

Horace   *'Scholars dispute, and the case is still before the courts.'*

◆ There are many different perspectives on leadership. The popular perspective is as valid as any other.

◆ Concepts and terms are plentiful. It is important to be clear about what the practical implications of leadership are and to share a common language when describing them.

◆ Leadership is more than the influence of one person's actions. It emanates from willing, inspired and motivated teams.

◆ Effective leaders adopt their leadership style(s) to suit context and demands.

◆ Naked ambition may secure the status of leader, but effective leadership is based on commitment to a vision, purposeful drive, the constructive use of energy, galvanising others and dedication to staff and students.

◆ Though there are different ways of describing 'professionalism in action', it is important to have in place a system to evaluate professional standards and to know on what evidence such evaluation rests.

3.1 Overview

To lead and manage change it is necessary to understand the culture of the school and how to sustain or improve this through the central mechanisms of planning and review. In addition, what the school expects to get out of any development has to be framed within a structure which takes account of the 'restructuring' which continually surrounds any school and the learning process. This restructuring has local and national elements. It affects the people, systems and resources which make up the school. There are fall-out effects on accountability, the structure and content of the curriculum, performance management and professional development. This chapter looks at some of these issues in the context of leading and shaping school development planning and the curriculum. The next chapter takes up the issues of performance management and professional development

3.2 The culture of the school

'The real voyage of discovery consists not in seeing new landscapes, but in having new eyes.'

Proust

The culture of an organisation stems from the pattern of basic assumptions it adopts. Its 'climate' or 'ethos' is shaped out of the attitudes, beliefs, norms and values which it espouses and attempts to reflect in its day-to-day provision and practice. In reality, the chosen and preferred way of 'talking and doing' is often more a 'best fit' consensus than true cohesion, since – as Notice board 4 illustrates – many viewpoints and values compete for recognition.

Notice board 4 Factors which influence the culture of the school

◆ Students' views of academic success.

◆ Norms of academic and other achievements.

◆ Parents' views and demands regarding academic success.

◆ Expectations of teachers and students.

◆ General standards of discipline, work and study habits.

◆ Overall level of commitment shown by governors, staff, students and parents. Predominant outlook on what can be done, e.g. capable of success versus pointless to try.

◆ Level of collegiality across the community.

◆ General quality of school life for students and staff.

◆ Overall state of morale

◆ Degree of stability versus disunity.

◆ Degree of control by vested interests.

◆ Clarity of goals and values.

◆ Degree of agreement or difference between national and local goals and values, and those adopted by the school.

From this profusion of influences, the leaders and managers in the school are expected to promote a sense of purpose and ethos. The level of success they achieve in this mission is usually judged against a range of characteristics. These include:

◆ a sense of community pride;
◆ respect for the rights of individuals;
◆ the promotion of equality of opportunity;
◆ sustaining traditions and experiences which attract loyalty to the school as a whole;
◆ relaxed, but effective systems, to maintain discipline and promote good behaviour;
◆ involvement of governors, parents, staff and students in reviewing and improving the school as a community;
◆ securing effective pastoral as well as academic care.

Ethos, and more especially the leadership's contribution to it, is not something about which valid judgements can easily be made. While one can compare intent with action (policy into practice), monitor and evaluate the *processes* which appear to contribute to the quality of the ethos (for example, attendance and behaviour, the rate and consistency of exclusions, the quality of teaching and learning across the age and ability range; staff–student relationships, the effectiveness of the pastoral system, the range of extra-curricular activities – and the amount of take-up; the general levels of attendance by parents and others at school functions, etc.), one cannot be precise on outcomes, nor on cause and effect.

> **Issues in focus 3.1**
>
> Inspectors usually make a summary judgement about the ethos of the school. They do so by drawing on conclusions reached from considering a wide range of evidence. In particular, they will focus on students' response to the school's provision – particularly its teaching, curriculum and the provision made for spiritual, moral, social and cultural development. They will also focus on the contribution of the school's leadership to the shaping of staff and student attitudes, relationships, the management of equal opportunities and the provision for SEN. Such judgements are inferential and indicative, rather than measured and absolute. In consequence, since the publication of the first inspection handbook, guidance to inspectors on how to collect evidence about a school's ethos has undergone significant revisions.

What is possible is to 'feel and witness' the character of a school, even though it may be difficult to sketch out the full range of contributing factors and their unique blend. By this largely intuitive process, it is generally recognised that schools with a truly positive ethos have several discerning features:

◆ they believe it is possible to shape the quality of human character;
◆ they give such work equal standing alongside that of academic development;
◆ they recognise and celebrate a wide range of achievements;
◆ they encourage students to take responsibility for others and to practise values;
◆ they model good practice in their handling of people and relationships;
◆ their programme of personal and social development is broader than just a commitment to cover cross-curricular issues;
◆ they enshrine this culture in their aims and policies and track the effects in practice;
◆ they make explicit the principles and values underpinning the life and work of the school;
◆ they believe everyone in the school should be life-long learners;
◆ they recognise that regular reflection improves practice.

The school's leadership cannot suddenly will this culture into existence. It is not on sale and it is not a set of transferable skills, like those a soccer superstar takes from one club to another. It has to be created from and maintained in the situations and relationships that comprise the school's normal day-to-day work. It emerges from a climate in which teaching and learning take centre stage; there is routine sharing of ideas, resources and practice; enquiry and problem-solving are natural events in the school's approach to professional challenge; there is individual and team recognition of the necessity to see jobs through; staff colleagues relate to each other and support each other in ways they expect students to, and senior and middle managers minimise the demands of administrative routines so that they don't get in the way of securing the school's *raison d'être*. Most important of all, the school frequently uses the 'eyes of others' to gain evidence on how its ethos plays out in practice. The insights of those not caught up in the daily hurly burly are used as stepping stones to move forward the school's continuous journey of strategic and scholastic development.

Issues in focus 3.2

Because the ethos of a school has a *surface* level that is relatively transparent and a *deep* level that is inwrought, improving the culture is not an overnight job or one that can be done by a talented task force in a matter of days. Though the parachuting in of a 'superhead' or changes in the management, staffing and resources may be an essential initial step to help pull round a school in trouble, the school will only respond and develop if the complicated set of actions needed to revive its spirit and fortunes are tackled in a sustained fashion. In areas where there is a great deal of family, social and neighbourhood dysfunction, this may mean help from the range of the education, social, medical and youth agencies, plus specifically targeted multi-agency initiatives, rather than just a general blunderbuss of change

In some states in the USA, such multi-disciplinary targeting is apparent in 'full service schools' and in Scotland there is some experience that 'one stop' centres make it easier to deal with many of the problems facing some schools serving difficult or disadvantaged areas. One stop centres seek to co-ordinate the efforts and resources of schools, health centres and neighbourhood social service teams into a combined and localised plan of support. The chief aim is not unlike that of the 'educational priority teams' of the mid- to late 1970s. It is to break into the culture of failure that takes hold of some families and some neighbourhoods. ↓

Even before the Excellence in Cities initiative was launched, some LEAs had identified school improvement zones for cross-school and cross-service projects targeted at particular concerns or needs, and some school consortia were working on common influences affecting their ethos and standards of achievement. Some of these initiatives have been successful in helping students to overcome barriers to learning. This indicates that in some situations, schools may only achieve a positive cultural milieu when they can address their needs within a 'supporting family' structure – i.e. a programme of constructive help within a cluster of schools, or within a schedule of sustained support from designated external agencies.

3.3 Planning and review

'Small deeds done are better than large plans left undone.'

Anonymous

The staff of a school and those who support them share responsibility for the school's success. Success has to be engineered out of what the school seeks to develop. Full success is planned for and the degree of success achieved is evaluated. This means there has to be concern with the practicalities and details of planning, but such planning has to be undertaken in a manner which is understandable by all, yet avoiding the pitfalls of exuberant blueprints, i.e. over-ambition and overkill.

A reasonable balance between intent and action is more likely if the school's leadership carefully decides what responsibilities it has for planning, and then considers how to bridge the difference between a *laissez-faire* approach, and an all-embracing, too time-consuming strategy.

There are perhaps six areas of responsibility which any leadership team has in respect of guiding and assisting planning. These are:

◆ creating, nurturing and sustaining the vision;
◆ clarifying the school's immediate, short-term and long-term objectives (as far as the latter can be forecast);
◆ advancing organisational structures to secure these objectives;
◆ recognising where best to make use of the different capabilities and contributions of team members who make up the school community;

◆ negotiating with colleagues and others who is to lead on what, and who is to be accountable to whom for which aspects of the overall development plan;
◆ determining how far development planning on paper is being seen in definite action on the ground.

All six areas can be integrated within the process of school-based review, especially if a clear cyclical process is established which links the stages of planning, review, evaluation and next development. Though cyclical and endless, the sequence is not necessarily easy to achieve, and it is seldom tidy and seamless. Hardie (1995) lists the principal characteristics of school-based review and Macbeath *et al.* (1997) and Macbeath (1999) outline the principal opportunities and constraints of school self-evaluation. McCall (1998) clarifies the essential difference between development planning and school self-review:

> *'The main difference between the two processes is that school development planning is essentially a statement of intentions. It is an arrangement to integrate the various aspects of school practice and planning. The plan offers direction (aims / values), sets the school in the context of policy implications (school, local and national), provides some indications of existing achievement, and offers some vision of future priorities. It is a mechanism for co-ordinating aspirations and intended strategies. School self-review on the other hand, is an activity-based programme of enquiry. It is the collection and examination of evidence and information on the school itself (or features of its work). The school is the subject of the review operation. The process of self-review helps to manage and verify the school development plan.'*

p. 44

Strategic PIN down – Reflection 3.1	Aim	
	◆ to audit the school's progress on the planning-evaluation cycle.	
	P – State the PROBLEM	Terms like strategic planning, school development planning, school self-evaluation, etc. can mean different things to different people. To avoid confusion it is ...
	I – Clarify the ISSUE	Some structures for planning and evaluation can be over-simple, mechanistic, uninspiring and ineffective. To avoid this 'downside' we need to ...

Strategic PIN down – Reflection 3.1 cont.

N – Tackle the NEED   Establish where the school stands in relation to the planning and evaluation cycle. Table 3.1 may help.

Table 3.1

Planning cycle	Whole school	Evidence	Students' achievements	Evidence
How well are we doing?				
How do we compare on a like with like basis?				
What more should we achieve?				
How can we make it happen?				
What is the first next step?				

Issues in focus 3.3

Any organisation needs clarity – clarity of purpose and clarity of direction – and schools are no exception. Creating a vision and establishing clear direction are key functions of leadership.

Effective leaders will be constantly examining their own values, beliefs, attitudes and behaviour patterns, as well as listening to others. The constant self-reflection results in a personal reference system against which individual leaders check policies and practices. Creating a vision and setting the direction for a school can be a lengthy process and might be co-terminus with creating a school culture of openness, trust, partnerships, teamwork and collegiality. It is within such a culture that a genuine shared vision and direction can be shaped. Investing in creating a collegiate culture is crucial, as is utilising and valuing the capabilities of staff.

In creating the vision and direction for the school, values need to be explicit and expressed so that all stakeholders can relate to them. While the vision will be challenging, it should also be capable of being translated into practice. The vision must be about change and improvement – though schools' mottos are usually about the past, a school's vision must be about the future.

> Leaders must have the ability and confidence to communicate a picture of this future and have the skills to combine the reinforcement of good practice with responding effectively to external demands. This requires constant referral to the vision and when necessary a redirection of priorities and targets to ensure continuous growth and improvement. If external pressures or changes have fundamentally shifted, it may be necessary to review the vision and strategy.
>
> Turning a vision and clear direction into pragmatic and inspiring outcomes is not unlike planning a crusade. There has to be sufficient conviction to rally and sustain followers, the identified values and priorities must be seen by them to fit with the current times and circumstances, there must be planned strategies, including contingent actions if declared objectives are not initially or consistently secured, there has to be practical logistics to get the armada moving, different people will be called upon to lead and facilitate different stages of the journey and operation, courage will need to be shown in the face of unpredictability and possibly hostile events, those doing their best will require comfort and recognition in the good and bad times, energy levels will need to be kept up, and when success is obtained, there has to be fair recognition of the individuals and teams who secured it and a fair sharing of the benefits. The call to the banner is about winning hearts and aspirations, but the crusade itself is a planned expedition. It is based on the best intelligence of what needs to be done and by what projected means.

3.4 Restructuring

Kronenberger

> 'The trouble with our age is that it is all signposts and no destination.'

We are all prone to resist change. We all have strong vested interests which reinforce this tendency. First, our security and status, earned through tradition, professional training and perhaps by long service may be threatened by revised goals or revised practices. Second, our professional work patterns may be so well ingrained that we sincerely believe there are no viable alternatives or improvements. Third, our personal and professional energies may be at a point where it is natural to resist changes that demand yet more from us. Fourth, we may seriously doubt the wisdom behind new initiatives and suspect that some of the claims made for a proposed change are based more on hype than substance. Fifth, we may see change as a possible source of conflict with others, which we wish to avoid. Sixth, we may lack experience with, and consequently confidence for, managing large-scale reorientation and development. Seventh, there may be an individual response to change – some proactively disposed people thrive on change, whereas reactives may naturally be obstructive to it. Eighth, change can be very differently perceived depending on the standpoint, i.e. issuing orders or persuasion from a distance, and being one of those doing the carrying out.

Schools are like all other organisations, They create programmes and strategies to repeat their successes. They have a tendency therefore to work more easily with modification, variation and fine tuning, as opposed to whole-scale root and branch clearance and replanting. Tension and the potential for conflict arise from the differences between the internal, measured reshaping, which is carried out by any organisation for its own purposes and at its own pace, and major radicalism which may be called for by those with the power to impose a powerful external agenda of change.

This tension and base of conflict are heightened when politicians and the society at large promote:

◆ inconsistent values;
◆ policies which conflict (or large goals which include inconsistent sub-goals);
◆ objectives or commands which are not readily demonstrable by those who espouse them;
◆ lost perspective;
◆ change so fast and so widespread that it creates a problem in its own right;
◆ large gaps between the ideals of a change and the finance available to move towards the aspirations envisaged;
◆ plenty of talk, but little real commitment to achieving the end result.

Despite the strength of such resistance and its understandable and even justifiable base, no organisation is inherently anti-change, and no school will thrive for long if it does not respond creatively to educational restructuring which arises from the combined influences of political mandates, inspection findings, research evidence and the profession's 'own voice' on how it should be responding to the educational challenges of a new century. The tricky task is to manage change so that stress does not go out of control and the change process in itself does not become an all-pervasive dependency state. This balance has to be maintained across several facets of the schooling process, including the staff and the curriculum.

3.4.1 Staff

It has often been said that staff are the most expensive and most creative elements of any organisation's resources. They have to be recruited in sufficient numbers to allow the organisation to be lean, effective and viable, yet by reference to some criteria which avoids the worst excesses of recent 'downsizing'. It is now generally accepted that the draconian downsizing movement of the 1980s and the 1990s has damaged the 'profile of expertise' in some organisations beyond the point of short-term repair, while at the same time destroying the corporate heart and pride on which service of good quality rests.

Although in the interest of value for money, cost-effective staffing quotas and flatter management structures are becoming more the norm, the staffing resource remains the biggest element of the budget. The manner in which the school staff is inspired or otherwise to carry out its professional commitment largely determines the ethos and effectiveness of the school. Equally, the professionalism of the staff also settles the size of the gap between the intended curriculum and what pupils actually learn. High expectations of staff and strong encouragement for their constructive efforts are indisputable influences upon professional application at the individual and collective levels, coupled with good lines of communication and effective deployment. Since failure to respond to necessary change may be calamitous for the school, leading and managing staff also embraces the capacity to apply sanctions and disciplinary procedures when the circumstances dictate that a colleague or staff team may need more 'push' than 'pull'.

Issues in focus 3.4

A number of schools now seek to ensure that all staff are more fully involved in the issues of staff recruitment, staff deployment, and staff discipline. The use of job descriptions divided into generic and specific sections, written policy statements on the use of learning support assistants and volunteers, working party information on issues such as curricular coverage and the range of teaching and learning styles, usually help to inform governors and senior staff of recruitment needs, including shortage of specific expertise and skills. ↓

Widespread involvement in the appraisal process helps to shape tighter assessment of the needs of individual teachers and the staff as a whole, thus informing recruitment and deployment, and a negotiated and clear rationale for staff deployment may circumvent irrational suspicions about unfair allocation of teachers, especially if the rationale is reviewed on a regular basis and not allowed to become a 'historical precedent' by default. Some larger schools use neutral and statistically-based types of staff deployment analysis, or they are advised by a staff deployment management group. National organisations offer planning tools which may assist corporate decision-making about recruitment and deployment – see, for example, the Audit Commission's (1986) advice on activity-led staffing. Negotiated codes of conduct in areas of professional sensitivity, e.g. governor visits, lesson observation and pupil shadowing, may prevent disharmony, while reminding everyone about the use of such evidence within disciplinary or grievance procedures, and several schools now have in their staff handbook an outline of the procedures used to prevent and manage staff conflict. For those new to headship, or a senior leadership function, the legal requirements and good practice features of staff recruitment and management are normally covered in LEA guidelines, or those produced by relevant phase or professional associations. It is essential for the school's leadership to understand the revised powers and duties of the governing body in deciding the conduct of the school and the school's accountability to staff.

In general, however, the majority of school staff respond positively to those mechanisms used in most organisations to encourage people to own the change process and to participate in it. Some of these are:

◆ *signpost* as far as possible, what the outcome will look like after the change has been completed; in particular, identify where the development is intended to change the school as an organisation (strategic planning; curriculum planning and delivery; the implementation of teaching and learning), but don't expect to have clear signposts for the whole of the journey and no caution or opposition;

'Nothing will ever be attempted if all possible objections must first be overcome.'   Dr Johnson

◆ *involve* staff in setting aims for the development, deciding methods to achieve the aims, and identifying criteria by which to judge the success of the project;

Inscription on Andrew Carnegie's tombstone

'Here lies a man. Who knew how to enlist. In his service. Better men than himself.'

◆ *frame* the intended development as a people-based / team enterprise and don't forget it; provide some visualisation of what is being attempted and timescale the development, e.g. place expected stages within the school's usual annual planning tools;

'Perhaps the key reason for the failure of management by objectives, is that the objectives are not thought of as the aims of the people. Instead we have those relating to "positions", "functions", or "departments" – all abstractions. The reality is people. Ultimately an aim is a self-guidance mechanism in a human brain. If it is to influence human behaviour, it must become the personal property of the team members.'

Scott and Rochester, 1984

◆ *research* options; explore the issues or challenges with staff before seeking to formulate specific strategies; use open discussion, brainstorming, and general opportunities to 'play around' with ideas; be open to novel suggestions; tolerate a degree of ambiguity;

'Halley, an astronomer, invented the diving bell; Dunlop, a veterinarian, the pneumatic tyre; Tull, a lawyer, the seed drill; a French priest the hydrofoil, and Booth, a bridge-builder, the modern vacuum cleaner – they were all specialists in other fields; perhaps they didn't know enough to know it couldn't be done!'

Smith and Ainsworth, 1989

◆ *distinguish* between 'can-do' and 'want-to-do' responses after this exploratory process;

C.D. Jackson

'Good ideas need landing gear as well as wings.'

◆ *demonstrate* the desired commitment and actions by 'walking the talk'; show consistency between managerial statements and actions;

St Francis of Assisi

'It is no use walking anywhere to preach unless our walking is our preaching.'

◆ *keep the pace up* by reinforcing commitment to the project and by regularly outlining the progress made and its value for students and the school community;

> *'Trust being lost – all the social intercourse of men is brought to naught.'*

Livy – Roman historian

◆ *emphasise collegiality* – 'everyone has something to offer'; 'we can discuss our differences'; 'we are right to feel good about this'; 'there is opportunity to share leadership and responsibility across this initiative';

> *'King Arthur's Round Table seated all its company on the same level. There was no head of table, and so no quarrels over precedence; mutual respect and reciprocal generosity were engendered. It symbolised the English tribal tradition of a leader as "first among equals".'*

Adair 1997

◆ *provide opportunities* for taking stock, testing insights and exploring possible developments and consequences;

> *'Authority flows from the one who knows.'*

Proverb

◆ *expect disappointments* since the process of development is seldom linear, continuously successful and without hitch; prepare staff for 'plateaux' in the development cycle; admit mistakes and revise alternatives;

> *'Innumerable confusions and a feeling of despair invariably emerge in periods of great technological and cultural transition.'*

Marshall McLuhan

◆ *evaluate benefits* within a problem-solving climate, i.e. outcomes are seen as productive areas for new investigation, rather than complete solutions or negative consequences;

> *'Others judge us by what we've done; we judge ourselves by what we know we're capable of doing.'*

Longfellow

3.4.2 Curriculum

Most of what has been written so far applies principally to the leadership and management of schools as organisations, and the processes within them of teaching and learning. The leadership of 'what is learned' is no less important. The personal fulfilment of the individual as a student and citizen, and the role of the school as a centre of learning excellence, depend on education leaders' skills to secure maximum curricular inclusion and the achievement of local and national learning targets.

Issues in focus 3.5

What might a 'centre of learning excellence' mean in practice? It is the process of creating, sustaining and promoting the school as a learning organisation with a learning culture. This includes:

◆ developing and sustaining a culture that is open; promotes trust and self-confidence; and where reasonable mistakes are an acceptable feature of professional development;

◆ creating a strong 'learning for all' policy;

◆ ensuring that commitment to learning is clearly articulated and reflected in all aspects of the work of the school – the vision, priorities, policies and practices;

◆ making all members of the school community responsible for learning – students, teachers, support staff, governors and parents;

◆ establishing systematic review and evaluation procedures, with regular focuses on the learning process and learning outcomes;

◆ encouraging close focus on evidence about students' learning, coupled with reflection by all staff on ways to bring about improvement;

◆ arranging continuous enhancement of attainment by regular, systematic and detailed reflection on where and why some students appear to be hitting the ceiling of measurable achievements;

◆ developing teachers' confidence to be 'experts' in the analysis and development of teaching and learning.

3.4.3 Compliance

Since the school is not entirely free to determine what curriculum it will offer, there has to be a structured and reflective approach to the school curriculum and the National Curriculum, including taking into account both statutory requirements and non-statutory guidelines. It is worth noting here that the strength of external constraints on the curriculum has varied over the centuries, but there have been few periods in history when schools have been completely free to decide the direction and emphasis of their programmes of study (see Interesting facts 3, page 53). This should not surprise us because, as an agency for educating all the nation's children, the school curriculum has to reflect the economic, humanitarian, religious and social goals of the society it exists to serve.

3.4.4 Application

Although the revision of the National Curriculum has resulted in a more explicit rationale for the school curriculum, and teaching requirements have been made clearer, each school's leadership has to contextualise the current design and structure so that the school's own curricular framework and the school's schemes of work effect a close match between central prescription and parochial needs. Indeed, the balancing of external demands and school specific contexts is the litmus test of effective leadership.

3.4.5 Equality of opportunity

The school has to establish how 'entitlement' will be enacted, monitored and evaluated in the development and delivery of 'its' curriculum. This has always been a priority and challenge for education leaders, irrespective of phase or socio-economic context, but with stronger emphasis from August 2000 on inclusion, the provision of effective learning opportunities for all students now has increased significance.

3.4.6 Uniqueness

The leadership has to decide how the curriculum flexibility which is available is to be used. This requires negotiation and agreement with governors, parents and the local community. Ideally, this consultation should lead to the development of a rationale and policy which, taken together, justify why the school has chosen to use the flexibility in the manner which it has. The school's leadership also has to draw up strategies for the evaluation of their curriculum to ensure it meets the needs of the pupils and the local community.

3.4.7 Match

There is a need to judge how far the curriculum does the following:

◆ reflects the aims of the school;
◆ is organised effectively;
◆ is broad and balanced;
◆ has content appropriate to students' ages and stages of development;
◆ contributes to the educational standards achieved by the students;

◆ prepares students for responsibility and the requirements of adult life;

◆ is enhanced by extra-curricular activities.

3.4.8 Intent into practice

The leadership requires a strategy to monitor how far the 'intended' curriculum (school, local and national requirements) is covered and delivered effectively in the 'operational' curriculum (the programmes of study and learning opportunities the students receive) and what curricular content and standards students' actually acquire (the 'achieved' curriculum).

The knowledge and skills required to carry out a curriculum audit or review are not onerous and systems for doing so are well covered in recent literature (see for example, Fidler (1996), Field *et al*. (2000), and Garwood and Dowden (1999). A pragmatic approach is to look at the curriculum as a whole, taking into account the means of its representation, delivery and impact. Notice board 5 illustrates such an approach.

	Notice board 5 Looking at the curriculum as a whole		
	Representation	**Delivery**	**Impact**
NC subjects	Use of NC handbook Use of Programmes of study School policies Schemes of work Timetable coverage Lesson planning	Subject expertise Quality of teaching and learning Differentiation within teaching and learning Continuity and coherence of terms and key facts across subjects/ departments/key stages	Attainment targets Level descriptions Statutory assessment standards Links with national qualifications
Other subjects	Place within school's curriculum framework School policies Schemes of work	As above + transfer between other subjects and NC, and vice-versa	Student's interest and confidence External examination results
Other aspects of the curriculum	As above + cross-curricular matrices	Intergrated work Team teaching Special points of focus or cross-curicular events	The development and use of the key skills across the school curriculum School proficiency certificates
General	Review formal decision-making arrangements and documentation	Track coherence and continuity Degree of student stimulus	Views of all key players Overall standards of attainment Value-added

Issues in focus 3.6

Some key indicators to monitor within a curriculum audit or review include:

◆ effective impact of curriculum planning on learning and achievement;

◆ pupils involved in profiling their attainment and experience;

◆ parents included as active partners in learning;

◆ governors involved in target setting, and the monitoring of learning outcomes;

◆ governors and staff establishing links between audit/review evidence and curriculum action planning;

◆ LEAs providing local schools' performance data for comparative, developmental and value-added purposes;

◆ account taken of the impact of learning resources, including the adequacy and deployment of accommodation and specialist facilities.

Interesting facts 3 The changing face of the school curriculum

◆ The earliest schools were annexed to, or part of, the foundation churches. Scholars studied *litterae* (grammar) or song (chanting – especially the Gregorian chant). After the conversion of Ethelbert, King of Kent, Augustine was allowed to establish his episcopal in the royal city of Canterbury. His missionaries taught Latin to the local priests and some nobles.

◆ In the classical period, the Church continued to provide much of the earliest organised education. It exercised complete control over the schools. The main object was to further the spread of the Christian faith.

◆ Alcuin of York (*circa* 766 on) describes an encyclopaedic curriculum built around seven liberal arts – grammar, rhetoric, logic, arithmetic, geometry, astronomy and music. This curriculum can be contrasted with the practical and mechanical arts practised by slaves, and then others (the manufacture of clothes, the making of weapons, the preparation of foods, etc.). This contrast between the liberal and mechanical arts was maintained well into the Middle Ages.

◆ Whether liberal or practical, the main concern of the early programmes of study was to assist students to acquire the contents of a prescribed course. For example, Latin and literature were the main studies in the medieval grammar schools, together with some instruction in religion and morals.

◆ Most of the charity and guild schools were affected by the anti-clerical revolution led by Henry VIII, but during the reign of Edward VI, a rising class of gentry, lawyers, merchants and yeomen did much through private contributions to retrieve the previous level of educational provision. In some schools, languages other than Latin and French, entered the curriculum. By the Elizabethan period, a number of undergraduates – such as Kit Marlow at Corpus, Cambridge – were able to exploit their interests in poetry and drama, though the general programme of education remained firmly clerical or quasi-monastic.

◆ By the 1700s, the common schooling of the upper and middle class was being criticised for its rigidly classical curriculum. Some academies, especially those in Scotland, were said to give their sons more 'broad and social book learning' than that received by the wealthier and idler English.

◆ In *Emile* (1762), Rousseau suggested the complete abandonment of a predetermined curriculum, with Emile being educated entirely through activities and by first-hand experience. This shift from predetermined content to a child-centred programme was not to take place in the UK for another 150 years, although direct influences on the curriculum, particularly those of the Church began to decline, as more schools endowed by wealthy individuals opened. Some of these institutions advocated a broad programme of study and methods of teaching based on encouraging pupils to observe and investigate.

◆ The monitorial system and the payment by results era confined both teaching methods and the curriculum. In addition, the costs of providing the meagre programme on offer were fiercely contested. For example, a Parliamentary grant in 1857 of £541,233 was regarded as an 'alarming increase' despite the total cost of the Crimean War to around £78,000,000. Ought the amount spent on education to be reduced? Was it well spent? In due time the latter question led to the introduction, and then strengthening, of school inspectors directly authorised by Her Majesty Queen Victoria.

◆ By the beginning of the twentieth century, the content of the curriculum, and the manner in which it was taught, was receiving close attention. In 1931, a Consultative Committee's Report *The Primary School* suggested the 'curriculum is to be thought of in terms of activities and experience rather than knowledge to be acquired and facts to be stored' – a statement which owed much to the writings of T. P. Nunn. There was also open debate and some disquiet at the secondary level, the latter illustrated in Lord Eustace Percy's 1933 declaration that the grammar school of the day was little more than 'a social factory for turning the sons of clerks and shopkeepers into clerks and shopkeepers' (Banks, 1955).

◆ Though the 1944 Education Act provided a clear vision of what system of education, and to some extent, what curricula would operate in post-war Britain, conflicting attitudes were still most prevalent, so that in presenting it to Parliament, its chief architect, R. A. Butler indicated that it arose from 'synthesis rather than consensus'.

◆ The post-war schools, more especially the secondary modern schools with their greater freedom from academic tradition, brought subjects such as 'commerce', 'civics' and 'technical studies' into the curriculum, and the Newsom Report (1963) in stressing that children needed to be 'socially aware' paved the way for later courses in the humanities and social education.

◆ Despite active work by HMI and the Schools Council between 1965 and 1977, in particular to develop a common framework for the curriculum and a pattern of curricular entitlement for all pupils, no consensus was reached, due in part to the competing pressures of a raised school leaving age, falling school rolls and local plans for reducing or re-organising schools.

◆ With these and other pressures came political concern about what the system as a whole was delivering, especially in terms of students' overall range of competencies on exiting school. Some thought that schools now concentrated too much on social concerns at the expense of academic goals, and students' vocational understanding and skills were considered to be too weak for the needs of the mid-1970s' national and world economy. The Prime Minister of the day (James Callaghan) called for a 'great debate' on education. This fuelled growing concerns about curriculum theory and practice, which in turn led to revitalisation of central control over the content and delivery of programmes of study. There was also a significant investment at this time into the application of microelectronics, and a centrally-funded range of initiatives to ensure this new technology and its implications entered the curriculum.

◆ The perceived 'mid-1970s' crisis in education' escalated in the early 1980s and a fresh look was taken at the content of the curriculum and the pattern of a possible 'core curriculum'. This was paralleled by an unprecedented shift in power over what schools did and how. This included greater parental choice, school competitiveness, published inspection reports on school performance, school specialisation, and finally the promotion and development of a National Curriculum for all maintained schools. In general, for many schools, curriculum development was essentially 'reactive' – planning to ensure they met legal requirements, including the implementation of National Curriculum assessment procedures.

◆ Curriculum 2000 continues the trend of a prescribed range of subjects with specified levels of achievement across different key stages. It also re-emphasises earlier expectations from the 1940s through to the 1990s, that proficiency in a range of key skills should be an outcome of curricular experience. Social goals are once again highlighted through the mandatory inclusion of citizenship. The promise has been made that the new curriculum will remain unchanged for five years in order to allow for a period of stability in curriculum planning and delivery. The maintenance of such a promise may depend on how rapidly the world changes in this time.

Strategic PIN down – Reflection 3.2	**Aims**
	◆ to describe how the curriculum operates in your school;
	◆ to identify what unifying effect the curriculum has on the school.

P – State the PROBLEM	Curriculum initiatives quickly become multi-faceted and widespread. To ensure co-ordinated development it is ...
I – Identify the ISSUE	A full-scale audit of the curriculum has to consider the school's academic and cultural goals, its human, physical and learning resources ...
N – Tackle the NEED	Internal key stakeholders require ...

Before you begin, decide:

◆ who the authors of the school's curriculum are;

◆ what sources of information are collated / will need collation;

◆ what natural planning cycles offer the best vantage points for reviewing the curriculum.

Reflection on the curriculum

Table 3.2

Issue	How the school's practice makes it happen
Multi-disciplinary organisation of the curriculum	

Strategic PIN down – Reflection 3.2 cont.

Table 3.2 cont.

Issue	How the school's practice makes it happen
Interrelationship of the different elements e.g. core content, key concepts	
Compliance with revised statutory requirements	
Ensuring equality of opportunity	
Consistent approach to planning and delivery	
Students' understanding of the relevant Key Stage	
Representation in schemes of work of permeative elements – e.g. economic and industrial understanding, environmental issues, etc.	
Students' progression	
Planned experiences for developing Key Skills	
Scrutiny of general resources and teaching materials	
Evaluation procedures	
Whole curriculum audit	
Stimulus for next stage curriculum development	

3.5 Summary

> 'Happiness is beneficial for the body but it is grief that develops the powers of the mind.'

Proust

◆ Changing a school requires an understanding of its culture and what needs to be sustained and improved.

◆ Changing the school's culture has to be based on a self-evident need and it must lead to real benefits. It is not an end in itself.

◆ A school's leadership need to be aware of the difficulties involved in changing culture, and to develop changes which are open, purposeful and as far as possible evolutionary.

◆ External perspectives can assist the processes of understanding the school culture and what needs to change.
◆ The change process is ongoing. It includes systematic and cyclical school-based planning and review.
◆ Resistance to change is likely to be less if school staff are active in deciding needs and involved in the change process.
◆ The school's curriculum is an integral part of its culture and curriculum development is a necessary element of the change process.

4.1 Overview

It is possible for an individual leader or manager, for example, a headteacher or head of department, to make most of the crucial decisions for their staff and to expect those decisions to be carried out. However, such a consistent autocratic style of leadership is rare in schools these days. This is because even the smallest school has a complex range of needs and these can seldom be met by one person's thinking and actions. The delivery of the curriculum itself demands the best use of each individual teacher's knowledge, skills and professional experience, and the majority of teachers are now expected to undertake multiple responsibilities and do numerous jobs. Many of these professional tasks require collaboration with others, rather than the discharge of isolated individualism. It is also increasingly recognised that the development of teamwork and the encouragement of self-managed teams enhance the school's capacity to function effectively in the temporary absence of one or more key players from the school, or the permanent departure from the school of a key member of staff. Thus, both within and outside of education, leadership which wastes the intellect, interests and practical skills of team members is now viewed with suspicion and mistrust. This chapter examines effective responses by leaders to teamwork, the development of self-managed teams and the use of collective decision-making. It continues by exploring the management of teachers' professionalism in the light of the possibly conflicting demand between the school as a communal entity, reflecting and modelling collective effort, and the confirmation that an individual teacher's work is beyond the performance threshold. The chapter concludes with a look at links between these concepts and the practice of effective professional development.

4.2 Teamwork

'Provide everyone with a stake in the outcome – if you seek a worthwhile outcome.'

Anonymous

Job advertisement
in a local newspaper,
February 1999

> **Notice board 6**
>
> 'We have achieved our success through a programme of change, with an emphasis on our staff working in small teams. To succeed in this environment you will need to demonstrate the initiative and determination to complete your work while being able to learn new skills. You will achieve this through your ability to effectively plan and organise your workload, and by being able to anticipate problems and provide solutions. Ultimately you must be a team player who can contribute to all aspects of the team ensuring that the needs of the clients are met.'

This description is fairly typical of the job advertisements now issued by commercial, educational, technical and public sector organisations. The modern emphasis is upon team activity, alongside the expectation that employees will acquire new skills and contribute to high levels of customer or client satisfaction.

This means that those leading teams have to motivate a collective response which sustains the team as a whole, keeps individual members up to scratch, and ensures that each individual in the team, and the team as a whole, develop the necessary people and technical skills to meet specified performance standards.

Such demands on leadership are likely to grow, as more schools are involved in job sharing, in the employment of part-time staff, in the use of short-term contracts, in different forms of professional networking and in the delegation of key responsibilities to self-managed teams. More than ever before, the principal leaders will have to fill a variety of roles, including those of mentor, supervisor and tutor. The ability to motivate very different types of teams is fast becoming the *sine qua non* of school leadership.

From the beginning, it is important to recognise that effective team work does not mask individual initiative and talent, quite the reverse. Team development grows out of and reinforces individual flair. There may also be within the team very different types of contribution. Some members may develop multiple skills and over time do any job the team requires; others may contribute specific expertise or be valued because they do certain tasks very well. In general, unlocking the power, skills and energy of people to work in teams requires the corresponding development of the team members as individuals. The two processes are mutually supportive.

An effective team is, however, more than the mere sum of the individuals who constitute the membership. There is a distinct difference between 'a team' and 'a group'. A working group may develop into an effective team, but just collecting together a group of people and calling them a team guarantees nothing. To be effective as a team, the group has to do the following:

◆ accept a 'team culture' which implies working honestly and fairly for the team, rather than for oneself;
◆ develop the capacity to work together and be prepared to learn as a team;
◆ work towards consensus decision-making, as opposed to citing individual preference;
◆ be open-minded about tasks and obstacles, including facing change and trying new ideas and methods;
◆ act responsibly together, without the need for headteacher or 'lead manager' supervision;
◆ be willing to explain and justify the team's manner and modes of working, and modify these as necessary;
◆ accept that teams, like individuals, are accountable for results.

Initially, it can be difficult to gain an appropriate level of team co-operation, and once in place, the cohesion, capability and achievement of the team have to be reinforced. It is also necessary to monitor the composition of the team against changing demands and circumstances, and either extend or alter the membership, or persuade the team to reshape the way it works, so that new challenges are surmounted.

The literature on how to build, use, sustain and improve team working is legion, see, for example, Adair (1986), Civil (1997), and Sergiovanni (1996). Overall, however, most authorities are agreed on the principal features which contribute to team success and team effectiveness. These features include:

◆ the team has a clear, accepted purpose, and this is published;
◆ it shares the vision, and is enthusiastic about its remit and priority tasks;
◆ it is drawn from people with good interpersonal skills;
◆ membership is representative of the full range of professional interests, balanced in terms of the necessary professional skills and powers of decision-making, and the age profile corresponds with that of the organisation as a whole;

◆ there is an early opportunity to explore differing views, differences of opinion and areas of possible controversy; this is coupled with the resolve not to allow any 'variance' to damage the team's spirit and its chosen *modus operandi*;

◆ there are open lines of communication to and from the team, especially about the nature of its work and the progress made;

◆ the team has within itself, or appropriate access to, expertise on project management and group dynamics;

◆ support structures are in place to handle significant conflict should this arise;

◆ the team has the ability to use both discursive and structured problem-solving tools;

◆ time has been set aside (within or outside of the working day) for the team to engage undisturbed with planning and/or development activities;

◆ senior managers openly recognise the value of the team's work and sustain this in the face of day-to-day routines and competing pressures.

Issues in focus 4.1

Motivating members of a team is a crucial leadership responsibility. Listed below are ways in which team leaders might motivate colleagues:

◆ acting enthusiastically yourself and being seen to persevere with tasks and challenges;

◆ showing that you trust individuals and the team;

◆ leading and managing by example and not by manipulation;

◆ treating team members as individuals – by regular dialogues that focus on higher-order needs;

◆ treating everyone in a fair and equal way;

◆ taking responsibility for mistakes as well as successes;

◆ acknowledging and praising achievements and building on them;

◆ avoiding public criticism of individuals;

◆ holding regular discussions about teamworking and ways to reinforce the team's purposes and outcomes;

◆ agreeing realistic and challenging targets for all team members;

◆ encouraging individuals to develop their capacities to the full;

◆ involving all members of the team (teaching and support) in planning and decision-making;

◆ ensuring that communications are two-way, open and frank;

- ◆ contributing to and promoting the personal and professional development of all team members;
- ◆ delegating as much as possible to individuals and sub-groups;
- ◆ giving regular feedback on the performance of team members and on any discussions with others inside and outside of the school;
- ◆ encouraging individuals to reflect on their practice, to share good practices and to learn from each other;
- ◆ providing opportunities for individuals to work together on a task and for colleagues to support each other in the team.

Not all teamwork requires leadership by or input from senior managers. Much can be achieved by delegation and the investment of trust in junior staff to act responsibly and with controlled enthusiasm. The key element here is trust, particularly reciprocal trust. Delegation involves the headteacher passing responsibility to another colleague or team, while retaining overall accountability. The parameters of the delegated task or role need to be clearly defined and the lines of responsibility agreed.

Issues in focus 4.2

Inspection evidence suggests that collaboration and teamwork are important contributions to effective school improvement planning (Ofsted 1994, 1995a, and 1999). The arrangement of adequate levels of consultation, focused group meetings, steering groups, working parties, team planning and collaboration across departments, phases or year groups are all identified by Ofsted as structures which encourage a consistent pattern of professional action across the school, and constructive responsiveness from staff to post-inspection requirements. Examples of successful teamwork include:

- ◆ governors working with staff to review the findings of inspection and to prepare a team-based strategic response;
- ◆ steering groups examining how best to assimilate post-inspection planning into the processes of annual forecasting and school self-review;
- ◆ collaboration and teamwork between heads of department to agree policies for improving some outcome, for example, the attainment of able pupils;
- ◆ teachers in primary year teams using assessment evidence for effective planning;

◆ using the specialist expertise of governors or external advisers to help existing school teams to meet specific objectives, such as a review of performance data;

◆ use of a working party to turn the outcomes of consultation into a draft developmental framework for approval by staff;

◆ a corporate enterprise to develop a post-inspection school self-evaluation strategy.

Strategic PIN down – Reflection 4.1	**Aims**
	◆ to list core values and guiding principles for a specified aspect of teamwork;
	◆ to consider the next steps in the development of the team.

Purpose of team ....

Priority objectives ....

Type of work (adaptation, innovation, next stage development, consolidation)

....

Representation needed ....

Time and resources to hand ....

Time and resources required ....

P – State the PROBLEM   There has to be the right level of motivation. This requires ...

I – Clarify the ISSUE   The range of experience and skills needed to respond is ...

N – Tackle the NEED   The team will have to learn ...

Values and principles cover sheet

When complete, insert on inside front cover of team's minute book, or similar.

Key question   Response

What do we as a team believe in?   a   Yes, we can do it!

b

c

d

e

Strategic PIN down – Reflection 4.1 cont.	Key question	Response
	What principles need to guide our co-operative work?	f There is always a better way. g h i j

Next steps in the development of the team
Place in back of team's minute book, or similar. Amend, as required.

Belief
IT CAN BE DONE

Somebody said that it couldn't be done
But we with a chuckle replied
That maybe it couldn't but our team would be one
Who wouldn't say so till we'd tried

So we buckled right in, with a trace of a grin
On our faces, if we worried we hid it
We started to sing as we tackled the thing
That couldn't be done, and we did it!

There are thousands to tell you it cannot be done
There are thousands to prophesy failure
There are thousands to point out to you one by one
The dangers that wait to assail you

But just buckle right in with a bit of a grin
Wave the team banner and go to it
Just start to sing as you tackle the thing
That cannot be done and you'll do it

Anonymous

Team development audit
Date when Working Towards is secured and transfer to Strong or Adequate column.

Feature	Strong	Adequate	Working towards	Secured
1 Outline of unique value team contributes to school.				
2 Optimistic outlook.				

3   Statement of purpose.

4   Commitment of time.

5   List of priority tasks.

6   Code of conduct.

7   Manner of working agreed
    (e.g. rotational or fixed
    leadership).

8   Communication arrangements in place.

9   Responsibilities clarified.

10 Possible obstacles to success identified.

11 Milestones/success criteria listed.

12 Initial action plan or progress chart in place.

13 Arrangements in hand to co-opt any needed
    advice or expertise.

14 Strategies to assist consensus decision-making.

15 Training plan.

16 Team review schedule.

17 Evaluation procedure.

18 Feedback arrangements.

19 Contingency plan (tasks, team membership, timescale).

20 Visible and continuing interest from self-managed team.

Review

Consider which features should be reviewed and prepare an outline action plan
to bring about any necessary changes.

4.3   Self-managed teams

Lao-Tzu

'When the best leader's work is done, the people say "We did it
ourselves".'

A good subject department or an effective teaching team usually has the
confidence and skills to operate as a self-managed team, even if they do not
describe themselves as such. Teachers working co-operatively to
complement their individual efforts, sharing efficiently the task of large-
scale planning, managing effectively a section of the school, or teaching
successfully together within some integrated programme of study are
demonstrating the capacity for organising themselves collectively and
directing their combined energies towards meeting specific professional
goals. Such expectation is becoming ever widespread.

'Perceptions among all managers within the sample were consistent inasmuch as there was a recognition of the trend towards flattened organisational structures with fewer layers of management within the organisation. Increasingly, interpersonal and social skills were seen as essential managerial attributes as management responsibilities were distributed more widely within the organisation, with day-to-day decisions being taken at the point of delivery. Managers were increasingly working within teams of people and aware of the need to ensure an optimum level of contribution from each team member.'

O'Neill, 1995, p. 24

The rationale for self-management is that societal and world problems are not going to be solved by people working in isolation. Every organisation and community group needs to engage to the full all participants' talents, skills, ideas and experiences. Inasmuch as the school is a microcosm of the changing world and the new culture, teachers working together to manage elements of the school's programme model for students the team contexts they will increasingly find as they take their place in the employment, leisure and social milieu.

Whole school management is not denied in the concept of increased delegation. However, it is thought of rather differently. It becomes the interlocking of self-managed teams as opposed to the more traditional linear 'top-down' structure. It is best represented as an interlinked series of ellipsoids or circles, rather than the hierarchical line-management diagrams used to illustrate more traditional arrangements. This is because a fair amount of the responsibility and decision-making is directly delegated to and invested in 'team units', as opposed to individuals holding senior or supervisory status. Teamwork becomes the core of the structure.

'When successfully implemented, self-managed teams have proven to be more effective than traditional work groups because they truly create teamwork. Most work groups do not operate like teams because each person is only responsible for their part of the job. In a self-managed team, if one person fails, the whole team suffers. Teamwork becomes a priority. Team members learn to hold each other accountable for doing whatever it takes to get the job done. ...

Members need to learn new skills (or use existing skills differently) to succeed as members of a self-managed team. These skills involve performing multiple work assignments. They also involve new ways of interfacing with each other and with people outside the team.'

Chang and Curtin,
1994, p. 6

Team self-management is not for a single activity, but a series of activities. It is a way of organising the school whereby the traditional hierarchy is 'flattened' to a certain extent, and the line from headteacher is direct to Key Stage team co-ordinators, heads of distinct school phases (lower, upper, post-16), or project teams (school-self-review, pastoral re-organisation, curriculum development, professional development), etc. There is team leadership, either by formal appointment, or with the leadership role being shared across the team by rotation. The crucial element is that a significant amount of decision-making and responsibility is passed directly to each team. They are expected to set up structures to handle these responsibilities and they are held accountable for their decisions. Such opportunities may well revitalise the school's approach to staff development as part of school improvement. For example, in a report on schools succeeding against significant difficulties, the National Commission for Education (1996) state:

> '[I]t is not essential to have new staff to create a new ethos in the staff room, and vigorous staff development had been used in preference to the replacement of teachers. Successful approaches involved knowing how to develop or "grow" staff capabilities, and acknowledging, in effective operational terms, the importance of non-hierarchical team
>
> p. 343   work.'

A move from a traditional structure to a network of self-managed teams cannot be done overnight. There has to be time to explain the rationale; convince governors, teachers, students and parents of the benefits; consult on proposed structures, and trial working practices. If the arrangement is to work successfully, team-building activities may be necessary before the full extent of delegation takes place. The team may also need time to develop professional language and documentation, so that these reflect the aims, objectives and mechanisms of self-management.

While not yet a proven system of effective school organisation, certain advantages can be put forward for self-managed teams. These include:

◆ increasing success in the use of these arrangements in commercial organisations and the public sector;
◆ less risk of self-chosen or circumstantial professional isolation;
◆ more team 'self-motivation', thus fresh thinking and new strategies are kept active;

◆ a shortened 'chain of command', thereby lessening the risk of decision-making being held up at too many 'check points';

◆ some freeing up of senior managers time from routine decision-making, allowing them to concentrate on strategic issues and broad professional tasks;

◆ a mechanism for operating 'mini-schools' within larger schools, thereby providing a closer reference point for students, staff and parents;

◆ earlier opportunities for staff to exercise managerial responsibility in their career, than some traditional structures allow;

◆ scope for tighter use of generic and specific performance indicators in job descriptions;

◆ more realistic governor-designation, since they are attached to less but more accountable team units;

◆ the co-ordination of development planning is across fewer key stakeholders and is therefore less likely to be piecemeal;

◆ visualisation and decision-making are more age- and phase-specific;

◆ the evaluation cycle is organised around more sharply defined core administrative and professional sectors of the school.

Members of self-managed teams tend to become so for a whole range of reasons. These include their willingness to participate in delegation, a belief that they can 'build up' to the task and hold skills beyond those they possess now, and a disposition to accept that most, if not all of their colleagues have relevant professional wisdom. Since the contribution of self-managed teams to school management is in an embryonic state, teams may need a programme of internal and/or external support, but they must be given the incentive of 'real challenges to manage' and proper mechanisms to advance their strategies.

4.4 Collective decision-making

> 'Fifty million meetings happen every day. They are one of the most common forms of communication at work. They are also probably the most expensive.'
>
> Alan Barker

The value that collective decision-making can have in the process of school management has been widely recognised, see, for example, Marland (1988), Wilcox (1992) and Ainscow *et al.* (1996). It is one of several core themes which crop up regularly in official and non-official educational publications. No matter what the process is called (consensus decision-making, team decisions, shared thinking, etc.), it is accepted as an essential element of democratic management, even though the use of it may be implicitly rather than explicitly stated, see Notice board 7.

Notice board 7 A sample of outcomes which rely to a large extent on collective decision-making

- a sense of ownership (e.g. school policies);

- community commitment (e.g. avoidance of bullying);

- active involvement of all (e.g. in the judgement process);

- collective perspective (e.g. learning goals);

- reconciling points of difference (e.g. quality of pupils' performance);

- sharing perceptions of success and areas for development (e.g. teacher appraisal, school self-evaluation);

- in-school review decisions (e.g. progress/placement of pupils with special educational needs);

- consistency (e.g. across schemes of work);

- shared statement (e.g. of educational values);

- agreed working practices (e.g. marking work, shadowing pupils);

- gathering and analysing information (e.g. by review group).;

- moderation procedures (e.g. of grades).

The responsibility for making a decision, and the task of doing so, may have to be retained by a leader acting alone if political considerations, matters of confidentiality, group disharmony or time pressures require it. In general, however, sharing with others the analysis and possible alternative courses of action leads to more effective decisions. Decisions made by consensus also have the advantage that because staff who have contributed to them feel they have 'been heard', they will tend to support the final decision, even if it has moved away from their original idea or opinion.

Issues in focus 4.3

In essence, decision-making is converting thinking into action using the processes of analysing, synthesising and judging. It requires imagination, conceptual ability and on occasions intuition. However, few decisions are made by a leader acting alone or in isolation from events and conditions in the team or the rest of the school. The profile of decision-making in a school will be congruent with the culture of the school, so that for example where there is openness, trust and collegiality this will be reflected in the decision-making processes and therefore crucially in the leadership and management style prevailing in the school.

Certainly, biographical sketches of past and present successful leaders and descriptions of successful teams tend to reflect their involvement in a high level of collective decision-making. This is not surprising, since most corporate decision-making has a number of distinct advantages. These are:

◆ visible and accessible process;
◆ individuals less exposed to shame and blame;
◆ the perceptions and convictions of those involved are usually revealed;
◆ possible pitfalls tend to surface or can be more readily anticipated;
◆ great range of professional experience and skills to call on;
◆ an agreed collective perspective provides the strength of consensus;
◆ chance to gain team spirit which acts to reinforce effort;
◆ more choices or options are identified;
◆ such action begins a process of co-operation which may be necessary to see a decision through to a successful conclusion;
◆ all participants learn and improve skills and hence expand the level and type of work they can do;
◆ process often results in a series of successful small steps, thereby promoting a positive professional image.

Despite the fact that collective decision-making is often regarded as desirable and seen to be more effective in the longer-term, it is not always easy to achieve. There are plenty of quips around to remind us that the level of challenge is steep. Notice board 8 displays just a few:

Notice board 8 Humorous thoughts on collective decision-making

◆ For God so loved the world, He didn't send a group.

◆ A group of three gets things done if two don't show up.

◆ Collective decision-making is a cul-de-sac down which good ideas are lured in order to be noisily strangled.

◆ A committee is a group of people put together to share the blame.

◆ Sign in a restaurant used regularly for committee lunches – 'Not responsible for loss of hats, coats, umbrellas or tempers.'

Nevertheless, collective decision-making is not just an ideal. At the end of the day, in settings as diverse as commercial, educational, social and political enterprises, it is the only type of decision-making that counts. In the end, if all are willing to work within the parameters of a decision, even if it is not their preferred option, a form of operational consensus is obtained. This may be the best position there is.

To get to operational consensus, a leader and team will draw upon a variety of human attributes. These will include intuition, practical common sense, convergent and divergent thinking. Different modes of thinking may be desirable at different stages in the process of making a decision, and in any decision-making team it is valuable to have people with different convergent and divergent strengths. It is also clearly essential that if decision-making is to be collective, the following points should be implemented:

◆ the team should be regarded as the principal resource and 'expert' – not an individual;
◆ working practices should not be over-directive, nor too mechanical;
◆ tasks given to the team should arise from real professional issues or concerns;
◆ timing and arrangements should generate the lowest possible levels of stress and the maximum openness;
◆ documentation or ideas presented to the team should be in 'draft form' and genuinely open to modification;
◆ information fed into the team should be clearly identified – e.g. opinion, evidence from observation or review, reflections by named source, and so on;
◆ professional challenge is presented as part of the 'working arrangement' and distinguished from personal dynamics;
◆ time is allowed to share differences of opinion and to create new viewpoints;
◆ strategies are available to divert the level of discussion, or course of thinking, if it becomes very negatively skewed or too anecdotal; (for more creative approaches to collective decision-making see Leigh (1993));
◆ when decisions are agreed, they are recorded and confirmation is sent to all members of the team;
◆ decisions made are publicly announced and ascribed to the team, not to an individual;
◆ if necessary, there is consistent and constant restatement of why the team is together and what it needs to achieve;
◆ time is set aside for the team to take stock of how it is working, to acknowledge the type and range of decisions it is making, and to assess their impact;
◆ evidence is regularly provided for the team of its influence and progress.

The identification of shared goals and priorities for collective decision-making is an important leadership function. Effective decisions will only be made in the context of a systematic approach to overall planning and development. Even though the decision-making process may be a very creative set of events, the focus of the creativity has to be the school's most pressing needs and its general strategic priorities.

4.5 Fields of operation

This combination of systematic focus and creative decision-making may well be helped if the decisions are related to the main fields of operation.

4.5.1 Preparation

> 'The future belongs to those who believe in the beauty of their dreams.'
>
> Eleanor Roosevelt

Deciding that a journey of accomplishment is necessary and then taking contingent decisions relating to what horizon or vision is being sought, what cartography is needed, how best to journey there, in what calendar time, who is to be in the team and with what responsibilities, what resources can be made available and how these will be deployed. Preparation of this kind will apply to creating the conditions for school improvement, developing the culture of the school, giving proper attention to long-term strategic planning, developing a response to inclusion, and building the necessary enquiry and reflection to engage meaningfully in school self-evaluation.

4.5.2 Process

> 'How far is far? How high is high? We'll never know until we try?'
>
> Special Olympics song

Decisions concerned with sustaining momentum along the route, how best to surmount unexpected obstacles, what modifications to make to pace and resources in order to allow for any delay, when to rest and take stock and when to press on, and what to do if the environment becomes inhospitable. The application of these decisions will apply to the differences between policies and practice, the opportunities and experiences students receive every day, the quality of teaching, students' levels of attainment and progress, and the school's evidence of value-added.

4.5.3 People

Charles Kettering

> 'No one would have crossed the ocean if they could have gotten off the ship in a storm.'

Agreeing decisions about what to tackle in teams and when. Deciding team objectives and how best to motivate the team members. Considering how best to handle time-management. Monitoring individual and collective stress. Exploring how to encourage individuals to improve their contribution. Deciding how best to handle the hesitant, or those who start to lose belief when the going gets tough. These decisions extend across staff deployment; the types of forums for meetings; the range and quality of professional learning; the involvement of staff, students and the local community in school policies and decisions; involving staff and students in information gathering about the life and work of the school; ensuring that people handle duties and data in a responsible manner; the nature and the quality of interactions between staff, between staff and students, and between sections of the school; the conduct of teachers, learning support assistants, students and volunteers, as they engage in the processes of teaching and learning; the involvement of governors and external agencies in school support and school improvement; the nature of the school as a social organisation and social experience, and the quality and impact of home–school partnerships.

4.5.4 Pay-off

Anonymous

> 'Fear of criticism is the kiss of death in the courtship of achievement.'

Deciding if the outcomes are worthwhile or to an acceptable standard. Thinking through how acceptable standards can be sustained with the present strategies, resources and levels of effort. Deciding if the perceptions and evidence about the quality of outcomes are fair and balanced. Monitoring co-operation between those who are responsible for the outcomes and those who receive the outcomes and their consequences. Preparing contingencies or rearguard actions if things don't turn out to plan, or if circumstances alter rapidly. Decisions of this kind will permeate the co-ordination of planning and outcomes; the effects of behaviour and learning contracts; the operation of key teams; the impact of professional responsibilities; the standards achieved in academic learning; the application of key skills and other achievements; the influence of outside help, and the general effects of delegation and collaboration.

4.5.5 Making decisions

In all these situations, if a decision is a 'choice between alternatives', then decisions made will depend to some extent on:

◆ the gathering of *information* to inform possible actions to take;
◆ the *justification* of the chosen path over other possible ones;
◆ the *firmness of mind* to go carry out a decision after it has been made.

Information might range from the broadly descriptive to highly complex data from statistical analyses. The leadership function is to help make sense of the information which is available and to steer towards using the information to good effect. This necessitates considering carefully the 'information chain', while posing and answering critical questions, for example:

◆ What information is held? What is used? Action plans, appraisal reports, budget and cost information, committee reports, consultants' reports, critical incidence analysis, forecasts, inspection evidence, parent feedback, performance data, psychometric test data, quality assurance information, questionnaire returns, research findings, self-assessment schedules, skills audits, student feedback, spreadsheets, strategic planning matrices, SWOT analysis, training needs analysis.
◆ Is the information relevant and up-to-date?
◆ Is it easily accessible? Or does it resemble the wit's definition of a filing cabinet? – '*A useful container where things can be lost alphabetically.*'
◆ Is it intelligible to those who have to use it?
◆ Does it flow freely to the right people and the right places? If there is no 'flow' – why not? For example, is a person or team knowingly or unwittingly 'shielding' information from others? Is there too much information, leading to 'silt-up' in the process of its analysis and use? Is the information too complex for the human or technological processing systems?
◆ Does everyone in the team have the incentive to ensure that the information pursued is purposeful and accurately collated?
◆ Does the information obtained and its manner of presentation contribute to both an immediate and longer-term view of options?
◆ In terms of the actual use made of the information which is gathered, is the chain a cost-effective sequence?

Presenting adequate *justification* for a particular decision (and course of action) stems from having real conviction that the decision taken and the ensuing strategies are based on a full and fair account of the contingent opportunities and constraints. It may include negotiating hard and straight on the pros and cons of the available options, and surmounting conflicts coming from the differing viewpoints of how best to proceed. In short, justification involves those in leadership roles, after giving time to the considerations by the team, setting out clearly what is being proposed and why it is the only possible way forward or the best-fit decision at this time.

Firmness of mind in sticking to a decision and seeing it through is not about heroic management, or presenting a tough culture, or showing the leader at the head of the cavalry. Indeed, if it is presented as one or more of these attributes, it is usually in order to show off an ego or to hide deep insecurity. Being firm of mind means being confident that the decisions taken, though not risk-free, are likely to achieve the desired outcomes. Accepting, therefore, that it will be necessary to reiterate the basis of the decisions for those who waver early, and to keep calm those whose natural pessimism may be too eager to call 'halt' before the consequences of the chosen actions are known. It is that moment of 'holding to course' because of faith in the decisions taken and a firm belief in the commitment and capabilities of those who have to carry them out.

How, then, might collective decision-making be assisted? Strategies could include the following:

◆ involving the key people or advisory groups in *focused discussion* or various types of *brainstorming*;
◆ sub-groups *role play* possible responses to a problem scenario;
◆ utilising diagrammatic and network systems such as *decision trees* and *critical path analysis*;
◆ testing possible courses of action by using *simulation*;
◆ clarifying responses to the group's thinking by having external *consultants* or members of staff who are independent of the process play devil's advocate;
◆ using *computer-based modelling* or *statistical probability*;
◆ matching objectives and choices by using *link matrices*.

None of these methods guarantees certainty of outcome. *The techniques do not make the decision.* They may point up particular choices, help with prioritisation, or show high risk factors – but at the end of the day they may make the decision-making process even more complex. The approaches have to be selected and used on a 'fit for purpose', basis.

Strategic PIN down – Reflection 4.2

Aims
- ◆ to consider collective decision-making;
- ◆ to apply it to a specified team or aspect of practice.

P – State the PROBLEM   Collective decision-making requires the acceptance of other people's views. This requires ...

I – Clarify the ISSUE   It is easy to end collective decision-making prematurely by ...

N – Tackle the NEED   The process is easier as more participatory decisions get made. To extend opportunity, we need to ...

Now complete the details in Table 4.1.

Area of application Team ....
               Task ....

Table 4.1

Aspect	Implications
C – Creating appropriate trust/climate	
O – Open structure/processes	
L – Leadership agreed or rotational	
L – Links/line management clear	
E – Effective framework to guide actions	
C – Communication arrangements	
T – Time phase determined	
I – Information/ICT back up	
V – Verification of role(s)	
E – Evaluative mechanisms in place	

4.6   Managing teachers' continuing professional development

'Education is the lifelong process of keeping your mind open to new knowledge and its application.'

Eisner

For any organisation, securing quality of service and securing high standards of achievement, resides in large measure on the vision, skills and commitment of the staff and those who train and support them. Active and sustained staff development is a direct investment in improving professional problem-solving and the work of the school as a whole. A motivating and systematic programme of staff development can serve to harmonise the various subject and professional interests which staff bring to their work, and serve to link the different organisational sections of the school. It will only fulfil these functions if it is 'fit for purpose' and leads to meaningful learning for those involved.

Fitness for purpose implies:

◆ a constructive relationship between the selected professional development activities and the identified needs which staff have to meet if they are to progress the school's aims and objectives;
◆ a close focus on enhancing students' learning;
◆ the use of opportunities and techniques which interest the staff, impact positively on their levels of motivation, and which are seen by them to be a valuable use of time;
◆ the improvement of staff knowledge and skills, or the acceptance by them of feelings or ways of thinking which improve their confidence and professional competence;
◆ tight links between the content and methods used for professional development and the range and levels of challenge faced by staff in their day-to-day work;
◆ professional development rooted in school-based, local and national processes of change;
◆ on occasions, meeting career aspirations as well as progressing the school's aims and objectives.

Leithwood (1990) provides an outline of professional expertise which is pragmatically fit for purpose in that it integrates both individual and school pedagogical needs, allows a degree of personal development planning, and is developmental, albeit in rather hierarchical terms:

◆ developing survival skills (knowledge about and limited skills in use of several teaching models);
◆ becoming competent in the basic skills of instruction (well developed skill in use of several teaching models);

◆ expanding one's instructional flexibility (growing awareness of the need for and existence of other teaching models, effort made to expand teaching repertoire);

◆ acquiring advanced teaching expertise (skill in application of broad repertoire of teaching models – professional plateau);

◆ contributing to the growth of colleagues' instructional expertise (reflective about non-competence and beliefs/values; able to assist others);

◆ participating in a broad range of educational decisions at all levels (informed, committed to school improvement, accepting whole school responsibility, able to exercise leadership).

The national professional standards (headteachers, subject leaders, SENCOs and SEN specialists) offer an alternative framework for auditing professional needs, prioritising individual and team professional development plans, and ensuring that professional development activities have a close relationship with individual, school, local and national goals.

For learning to be meaningful, those engaged with it have to be convinced that it will do the following:

◆ meets their agenda of personal and professional development;

◆ leads to greater levels of professional satisfaction and professional progress;

◆ helps them to cope with continuous cycles of change;

◆ helps them to meet more effectively the needs of any staff they may have to train or support;

◆ enables them to apply their learning to practical situations, especially improving students' learning and behaviour;

◆ provides information, ideas and resources which retain a reasonable 'shelf life'.

Issues in focus 4.4

Well-structured school improvement processes offer a myriad of opportunities for professional development – by encouraging self-reflection, by identifying specific tasks and individual development needs, and in some instances by releasing resources. The clear and sustained focus on school improvement has in many cases created cultures that value collaboration and thereby encouraged staff to share expertise and to work together. In such a culture leaders support staff in meeting school and career goals, recognise and celebrate staff achievements, and highlight that the professional development of all is a major contributor to raising standards in the school.

Professional learning, both individual and team, is most effective when integrated with everyday practice and when it forms part of a learning culture which permeates the whole school. Schools as learning organisations were briefly considered in Chapter 1, and West-Burnham and O'Sullivan (1998) and Ainscow *et al.* (1996) concisely cover the concept. But since members of the school community learn, not the school, a 'learning culture' is an essential stepping stone to the school acting as a learning community.

The minimum conditions for an effective and efficient learning culture may be summarised as follows:

◆ the attitudes and behaviour of senior managers reflect a belief that all learning by staff is valued;
◆ they actively promote individual professional development within a targeted and progressive programme of school development;
◆ like other aspects of the school's life and work, professional development is tackled as a strategic enterprise;
◆ institutional review, individual appraisal, the viewpoints of governors, parents, staff and students, and any evidence about the school's overall performance are used to decide focus and initial direction;
◆ what can be planned in advance, is planned;
◆ the professional learning process is a managed affair, key roles and responsibilities are identified and assigned;
◆ professional development needs are assessed, forecasted and costed;
◆ a close eye is kept on the effect that training and other aspects of professional development is having on daily needs and the core targets set out in the school's mission statement;
◆ evaluation of the process and outcomes of professional development feed into the next stages of the school's development planning;
◆ the school celebrates achievements which arise from the programme of professional development, thereby reinforcing staff motivation through public acknowledgement of success;
◆ staff are encouraged to adopt a '3Rs' approach to professional learning, namely,
    – engage in it *regularly*;
    – pursue it *rigorously*;
    – and *report* it back for the benefit of colleagues and the school overall;

◆ the school is regarded as an ongoing research-based learning
environment, since:

– there is a proactive approach to the future;

– action-based research is used to address more endurable problems
and challenges;

– ideas are encouraged and explored;

– there is tolerance of relevant enquiry and risk-taking;

– though the school seeks and expects success, error is allowed for
and blame is treated as a corporate issue, not a matter of individual
failure;

– there is acceptance of the necessity to cope with periods of
uncertainty and ambiguity.

Issues in focus 4.5

As stated earlier, professional learning has to be set in the context of school-
based, local and national changes. These are ever shifting points of focus and
the only realistic way of dealing with them is to encourage the 'transformational'
rather than 'assembly line' approach to applying change. The former implies that
directed change is assimilated into one's own educational values and priorities,
through teachers' application of critical acumen to the best manner and means
of adapting to the requirements, so as to benefit their pupils and their school,
much as they would encourage their students to respond personally to political,
social and ethical changes. The assembly line approach is an instrumentalist
view, which sees new developments as pieces to be added to the line, the
teacher's job being to fit them in as instructed. Such an approach suggests
simple, 'right solutions' to the complex matters with which schools have to deal.
The approach has not been successful in its previous guises, nor is it implied in
the recent DfEE consultation paper on support for teaching and learning

*'We want to support decision-making by schools and teachers and help
schools to become learning organisations.'*

In Annexe 2 of the same consultation paper a proposed 'code of practice' for
professional development states that high quality professional development will
do the following:

◆ meet identified individual, school or national development priorities;

◆ be based on good practice – in development activity and in teaching and
learning;

◆ help raise standards of pupils' achievements, including those with special
educational needs;

*Overview to
consultation paper
on Professional
Development
Support for Teaching
and Learning,
DfEE, 2000*

- ◆ respect cultural diversity;
- ◆ be provided by those with the necessary experience, expertise and skills;
- ◆ be planned systematically;
- ◆ be based, where appropriate, on relevant standards (e.g. subject leaders, SEN, SENCOs);
- ◆ be based on current research and inspection evidence;
- ◆ make effective use of resources, particularly ICT;
- ◆ be provided in accommodation which is fit for purpose;
- ◆ provide value for money;
- ◆ have effective monitoring and evaluation systems, including seeking out and acting on user feedback to inform the quality of future provision.

What hopefully will be integrated successfully as the government seeks to raise the status of the teaching profession is the apparent imbalance between team and individual performance in the new pay scale arrangements, the links between specific appraisal targets and pay, the continuing use of national professional standards, and the distinct, yet inevitably interrelated roles to be played in teachers' continuing professional development by the DfEE, General Teaching Council, and the National College for School Leadership. The need is for a considered continuum of professional growth, mapped in the form of a consensus framework, and with points of access at the level of the school and the individual teacher. Such a framework needs to encourage school self-development, practitioner reflection, and within and across school collaboration. It also needs to incorporate the concept and practice of Advanced Skills Teacher and guide this role in a manner which encourages the development in schools and school consortia of purposeful professional learning teams. Field *et al.* (2000) explore how these new initiatives and structures may impinge on curricular issues and teachers' personal career development. Whitty (1999) explores some implications of 'professionalism in new times'.

In general, the increasing central commitment to professional development may enhance opportunities for school-based research and for teachers to develop as reflective practitioners, or it may lose focus and strength across tightly applied pay structures, the numerous recent educational initiatives, and the possibly conflicting roles of the new professional development agencies. The best line of action is to engage proactively with any opportunities there are to shape the agenda.

Interesting facts 4 Teachers' initial and continuing professional development

◆ The first rating scale of teachers' professional competencies and their essential human qualities was probably introduced before AD 90. For example, the Roman orator Quintilian in describing his 'ideal teacher' laid down those aspects of character, morality and intellect he considered necessary to do the job. He also indicated features of pupil management and teaching method, which the ideal teacher should develop.

◆ The Jesuit educational system (*circa* 1530 on), whatever its faults, reinforced the idea of a cultured and highly-trained teaching profession.

◆ Pestalozzi through his institution at Yverdon (1805–1827) insisted that teaching should follow an orderly sequence and be based on secure and learnable principles and practice. A number of eminent scholars visited Yverdon, among them Froebel and Dr Charles Mayo. Mayo and his sister Elizabeth came to appreciate the strengths and defects of Pestalozzi's teaching and Elizabeth later put these and other observations into practice in her work training teachers at the Home and Colonial Society's training establishment.

◆ Also during what has become known as the 'age of philanthropy', David Stow developed his 'training system'. Stow arrived at this after working among the poor of Glasgow and developing his 'Sunday School'. Through his own thinking and his debt to Pestalozzi, John Wood and Samuel Wilderspin, he negated the 'monitorial' system of teacher training and insisted that *'an apprenticeship is as requisite for the profession of schoolmaster, as that of any other art'* (Stow, 1840, pp. 30–1). In general, Stow's ideas and his 'trainers' had significant influence upon the elementary schools of the 19th century. John Wood through his experiences at the Edinburgh Sessional School also extolled the benefit of a teacher trained in his 'craft'.

◆ The beginning of state intervention in education (1830 onwards) pressed forward the idea of a training-school for teachers. This led to the colleges of St Mark's and Borough Road – both in London. Dr Kay, later Sir James Kay-Shuttleworth, maintained the attack on the monitorial system calling it mechanical and 'monitorial humbug'. He believed that pupil-teachers should serve an apprenticeship under the guidance of an experienced headteacher, and then train for the profession. Kay and a friend opened a training college in Battersea in 1840 but by 1842 they had mounting debts. The college was handed over to the National Society and the notion of 'training colleges' for all teachers was sown. Between 1843 and 1845 the Church established around 22 such institutions. Kay-Shuttleworth went on to develop an influential scheme for training teachers (1846) and at the same time those wishing more religious connections continued also to open their colleges, for example, Homerton also opened in 1846. In 1856 the training programme was fixed at two years.

◆ The first entrants to training were largely 'pupil-teachers' but by around 1921, most intending teachers passed direct from secondary school to college. From 1904, those intending to teach 'pledged' to teach in a recognised school for a designated period after training (seven years for a man; five for a woman). LEAs could develop their own colleges and 'municipal colleges' opened in many of the big cities. Wholly residential colleges and subject specialist colleges were in place by the outbreak of the Second World War.

◆ Planning for the aftermath of war saw the launching of the teacher 'Emergency Training Scheme' (1943). This sought to recruit men and women from the armed services and the colleges offered a 'one-year' intensive training programme. There was also an expectation that after training these teachers would follow a course of 'directed reading' to improve their academic knowledge. The scheme was ended in 1951 and initial training reverted to two years. It was extended to three from 1960. The overall theme of initial teacher training in the 1960s was that of expansion; 40,000 students were in training by 1961; by 1971 this had become 120,000.

◆ University Institutes of Education began to develop from 1946 and 'refresher courses' and those for study beyond the first certificate began to develop more rapidly than hitherto. From 1969 onwards there was further close scrutiny of the organisation, structure and content of teacher training. A Committee of Inquiry was set up under Lord James and their six objectives (James Report, 1972) met with near universal acclaim. One objective has almost been secured (that of an all-graduate profession) and a second (planned reinforcement of initial training through induction) has met with a degree of success. Systematic expansion of in-service training has only been partially secured and the control and co-ordination of teacher supply are still a perennial problem.

◆ Teacher training numbers were halved in 1981 and the 160 public sector colleges of 1972 became 70 by 1984. HMI reported in 1982 that there was too little consistency across teacher training and they expressed concern that teacher employers had no guarantee that an agreed and consistent professional preparation had taken place. In 1984, the then Secretary of State for Education used (Teachers) Regulations in new ways. Course approval was put on a centralised footing and the later

Council for the Accreditation of Teacher Education (CATE) introduced a particular view of teacher competence. Tighter controls followed on both initial and in-service teacher education. INSET also widened from a 'going on courses' base to a variety of different types of professional activities. More school-based training developed, much of it centrally driven, alongside a growth in accredited short courses and modularised patterns of advanced diplomas and higher degrees. Monitoring and assessment of the effectiveness of initial and in-service education continued to be tighter with appeals and strategies to secure more rigour. As yet, no fully satisfactory means of assessing the effectiveness of teachers' professional development has emerged and there is not yet consensus of how effectiveness should be determined.

◆ The signs, however, are promising. In general, the largely 'unmanaged, uncoordinated, *ad hoc* and reactive INSET of the 1980s' is developing into a 1990s' *'rolling programme of "professional development" within a stated development plan at school LEA and government levels'* (West-Burnham and O'Sullivan, 1998).

◆ The work of the Teacher Training Agency and others to develop a coherent framework for continuing professional development has led to the current DfEE draft consultation document 'Professional Development: support for teaching and learning'. Though the broad principles and the tone of the document have been well received, there is healthy scepticism on matters of funding, the role of higher education institutions, the place of academic research and the balance between the process of professional development and its outcomes. In general, teachers' professional development continues to be a 'watch this space' scenario.

4.7 Summary

> 'For free will does not mean one will, but many wills conflicting in one person.'
>
> Flannery O'Connor

◆ There is an increasing emphasis on teamwork in managing schools and the teaching and learning process.

◆ An effective team rarely appears, it is built and shaped over time.

◆ Effective teamwork is an important element in planning school improvement and meeting post-inspection requirements.

◆ Several organisations, including schools, are changing their management structures to give greater scope to self-managed teams.

◆ Collective decision-making allows for the identification of shared goals and priorities.

◆ The process of collective decision-making gives several people a stake in 'making it happen'.

◆ Working collectively to make and implement decisions about the school's development is a valuable form of professional learning.

◆ Teachers need high quality professional development. This needs to be fit for purpose and framed within a positive learning culture.

◆ Schools are at the heart of a major programme of educational change. It is easy to feel left 'swimming in recommendations'. It is important to ensure that professional development adopts a transforming rather than accepting/functional approach.

5.1 Overview

Individual and collective leadership is more than the application of a set of professional skills. Leadership must be visionary. Leaders must hold some idea of the distant horizon and full game plan, and they need the capacity to maintain personal and team momentum on the journey towards securing the desired goal. They must also show rich human qualities such as an allegiance to a mission, curiosity, daring, a sense of adventure and strong interpersonal skills, including fair and sensitive management of those who work with them. They must be able to motivate themselves and others, demonstrate a commitment to what they espouse, release the talents and energies of others, have strength of character, yet remain flexible in attitude and be willing to learn new techniques and new skills.

Few people possess all these characteristics at one time, and even fewer people can fulfil and maintain all of the different roles which leadership brings. This is why the promotion of collective leadership, including the development of self-managed teams, is an important aspect of organisational management. Collective leadership is far more than meetings to determine the central prescription of rules and structures by which to make decisions and manage the school. At the heart of collective leadership is an enabling process which involves groups of staff in real management tasks, as opposed to just organising them into loose administrative confederations.

The most caring, effective and efficient teams tend to share out the demands and strains of leadership. Such groups also create a climate conducive to leadership at all levels, since there is natural acceptance that all can and will lead to some degree, as circumstances require. They also develop a corporate approach to managing the anxieties and stresses which arise in the day-to-day work environment. This chapter looks at the principal elements of this climate – namely, team motivation, team cohesion, conflict resolution and the management of stress.

Interesting facts 5 Individual versus collective leadership

♦ Harvard Business School once offered a course designed to teach 'followership'. Only a few per cent of those eligible entered. On the other hand, a course on 'leadership' attracted nearly 100 per cent.

Duke 1988

♦ The popular statement – 'autocracy breeds mediocrity down below' – is attributed to Michael Shea.

♦ Back in the 1960s, Massachusetts Institute of Technology studied the effects of communication and team structures on the speed and effectiveness of decisions. Broadly speaking, the more difficult the competing choices and information, the more hierarchical arrangements tended to 'silt up' because all communications had to go through the top. They experimented with 'star shaped', circle and 'circle-linked' forms of organisation. In general, flexibility and sharing seemed to be important facets in making quick and harmonious decisions.

♦ Illustration of the loneliness of leadership in a tight hierarchy: *'It often happens that I wake at night and begin to think about a serious problem and decide I must tell the Pope about it. Then I wake up completely and remember that I am the Pope.'*

Pope John XXIII

♦ Back in the thirties, the late anthropologist Ruth Benedict studied the Zuni tribe – part of the Pueblo Indians of Mexico. She contrasted their group-mindedness with that of rank individualism in other groups. For example, a man who had built a house or raised a crop and who, for some reason then had to leave the pueblo, had no feeling of loss – he'd worked for the group; also a death was mourned not for its personal associations, but because the group had lost a member.

Patterns of Culture

♦ A pharmaceutical company had excess capacity on a blister-packing machine. A team was posed the question 'How to utilise the blister-packing machine more efficiently?' Slip-writing was used to trigger brainstorming. One idea which emerged was a unique wash system (and pack) for contact lenses. Sometimes a 'good idea' starts very distant from the organisation and its immediate problems.

Quoted in Smith and Ainsworth, 1989

5.2 Team motivation

> 'It is difficult to inspire others to accomplish what you haven't been willing to try.'

Oscar Wilde

Motivation is a complex and ever-changing state. Individuals and teams display subtle differences. There is no definite or single set of rules or procedures which guarantees their motivation and commitment. Hence, there is no single technique or quick fix strategy to improve team disposition and performance. Equally, there is no guarantee that the *willingness* and *team spirit* which is optimal in the team today, will be sustained in the immediate and longer term.

It is also important to recognise the personal side of motivation. Most of it is intrinsic and private. It is an inferred rather than accurately measured phenomena. An evaluation based on considering just the external features of behaviour is not always a reliable indicator of a person's energy, drive and true enthusiasm. An individual's past success (as a proxy for their state of motivation to reach new achievements) is not a firm predictor of their future performance.

All these features of motivation need to be borne in mind by those charged with achieving team cohesion and success. Most leaders need to know the established 'bulletin board' facts about motivation. These come from different types of information. Some has been passed down over the years from day-to-day experience, some arises from the findings of social science research, and some has emerged from the wisdom of those who have managed to motivate successful teamwork.

Notice board 9 The motivation billboard

◆ A lot of motivation stems from self-awareness and self-perception. People are most likely to take advantage of opportunities to increase their skills and knowledge, to improve their competencies, and to contribute to team effectiveness when they are encouraged to reflect on how their own strengths and needs will benefit from team endeavour.

◆ There are several helpful theories about the nature of motivation, see Adair (1986); Berne (1964); Kelly (1955); Maslow (1968); McGregor (1960) and Mischel (1984), but the actual practice of motivating people has still, to a large extent, to be based on intelligent trial and error.

◆ The best that leaders can do is to create the conditions under which people become self-motivated. Such creation depends on leaders and managers being able to motivate themselves. It is also based on knowing people's strengths and needs.

◆ Standardised tests of motivational states have low reliability and suspect validity (Kline, 1993). In general, more research and development is needed before such tests are readily accepted as indicators of sustained motivational states or drives.

Some years ago a survey was carried out to identify factors people mentioned as either a positive or a negative force on their professional disposition and work. Those factors associated with high morale (sense of achievement, recognition of ability, interesting work to do, responsibility and promotion prospects) were called *motivators*. Those factors seemingly less connected with high morale (earnings, boss's attitude, work conditions, boss's technical skills, and the effects of policies, administration and communication) were termed *hygiene factors* (Herzberg, 1959).

> *'It is extremely important to realise that in separating these things Herzberg was not indicating that the hygiene factors were unimportant. Their effect on people is, if you like, something similar to the nature of a sewer. When it fails to function properly it becomes extremely important for everyone in the vicinity that it should be put in a satisfactory working order as quickly as possible! Once it is done, however, it quickly fades from memory of the people concerned and no longer as any effect on them. As long as the sewer continues to work properly, improving its efficiency still further will have no beneficial effect on those living around it.'*

Scott and Rochester,
1984, p. 109

As Scott and Rochester point out, Herzberg later softened the line between 'motivators' and 'hygiene factors' and agreed they may work differently at different times in society and within different value systems. Nevertheless, other researchers have since sought to discover what factors people regard as influential on their motivation and to what level, and their findings have some similarity with those originally proposed by Herzberg (see Issues in focus 5.1).

Issues in focus 5.1

A study of 35,000 employees for the Economic and Social Research Council looked at job satisfaction levels in different professional occupations. Surprisingly, jobs with the highest levels of satisfaction were often service sector jobs with relatively low pay. Top jobs for top satisfaction were medical secretaries, clergy, child-care professionals, farmers, education assistants and restaurant managers. Unsupervised working, flexible hours, doing something useful and lack of stress seemed important factors in job satisfaction.

In contrast, people in telecommunications, civil service executive officers, construction workers, quantity surveyors and printing/publishing agents were among those reporting lowest levels of job satisfaction.

The research highlighted two broad types of satisfaction. *Material* satisfaction – related to money, promotion, and security, and *quality* satisfaction – the nature of the job, the hours and their flexibility and the relations with the boss. Many jobs scored high on one and low on the other (LMI, 1999).

It seems there is a rough hierarchy across factors which contribute to high morale. Thus, beyond a certain threshold, pay and conditions are not the primary contributors. Equally, once a reasonable administration is in place, spending time on improving the 'efficiency of the school and the orderliness of its systems' may not be as important as spending time in providing adequate support for staff's professional and welfare needs. Headteachers who look to staff development responsibilities as much as to administrative ones may find this is itself a prime key to staff motivation.

'*My earlier incarnation as staff developer was one in which I imposed expectations on teachers, and compliance lasted only as long as I was there to monitor and supervise. Change that emanates from teachers, on the other hand, lasts until they find a better way. And perhaps the most welcome discovery for me was that the life of a school principal who redefines his role as staff developer can become quite rich and satisfying.*

I find that staff development is least effective when planned, premeditated, and deliberate. When principals set out to train teachers, run workshops, conduct inservice training, or direct faculty meetings, I see only modest professional change come to teachers. On the other hand, I find professional development most likely to occur as a consequence of teacher and principal pursuing regular issues and functions together.'

Barth, 1990, p. 58

Other important keys are finding where people's self-interest and professional interests lie. Though it may be easier now with highly refined oil to purchase one type to suit many mechanical functions, one approach to staff, or just one type of incentive for all is too restrictive to keep the many cogs in a school's dynamics running smoothly. This means there cannot be a blanket response to staff motivation. It is essential to seek some understanding of the unique set of needs which motivate each individual.

> **Issues in focus 5.2**
>
> Leaders might also reflect on how they are motivating themselves. The following questions may be helpful:
>
> ◆ Am I still committed to the goals and objectives of the team?
> ◆ Am I leading by example and sharing my strengths?
> ◆ What are my 'unique set of needs' which motivate me as a leader?
> ◆ Am I trying to motivate others?
> ◆ How am I making a difference?
> ◆ In what ways have I helped members of the team to make progress, complete a task or project, or gain promotion?

To motivate a sports team, the good manager gives demonstration and shows examples in the training phase, directs and encourages when possible from the sideline, but provides maximum latitude to each individual player and the team as a whole when they are engaged in the event itself. Equally, if the action is not going to plan, there is guidance on what each member of the team might do differently, plus a rally to team spirit and to the call of 'we' rather than 'you' or 'I'.

In general, factors that facilitate staff motivation, work effort and team action are not dissimilar to those which staff use with students. Everyone responds to the following:

◆ respect and liking;
◆ intrinsic and extrinsic rewards – shifting, as with students, over time to more internal motivation and learning for its own reward;
◆ an interesting or novel challenge;
◆ different levels of arousal (sufficient concern/tension to gain attention and application – but planning to avoid tension overload which impedes or arrests development);
◆ regular and balanced feedback; accepting that, just like the students, the school community needs knowledge of results;
◆ match for success – that is, attempting as one would with students, to provide work and challenge at a level appropriate to mood and capability.

Another dimension of thinking is to garner the main wisdom on motivating staff into a set of key statements like those which follow:

- accepting that teachers, like most people, 'work to live', not 'live to work' – finding, therefore, the best balance that can be achieved between what has to be done and the creation of time within and outside of school to enjoy a rich and stimulating life;
- senior managers and teacher-leaders personally demonstrating people care, as well as outward confidence, commitment and considered strategy;
- demonstrating that management has a duty to the staff as well as the other way round;
- reducing to the absolute minimum hierarchical management structures, coupled with genuine efforts to develop a larger team culture;
- abandoning any 'stick and carrot' approach and replacing it with the recognition that high morale, coupled with the will to achieve goals are the centre pieces of team motivation;
- after consultation, setting down a policy indicating how growth will occur in the opportunities for staff to be involved in running and developing the school;
- being clear and fair with staff about what 'power arrangements' are in force, for example, not letting staff think they are able to make and implement decisions, when all along the intention is to give others the final say; or appearing to seek views and collaboration, but actually ignoring them when 'push comes to shove';
- making flexible use of creativity and intelligent trial and error, to set up conditions in which the concern for the individual is demonstrated within an ethos to do well by the school and the students it serves;
- being explicit on what tasks need to be done, and possibly offering a first method or approach, but equally encouraging staff to find their own ways of meeting the requirements;
- building into the school routines as many motivating influences as possible – in particular, making effective use of individual talents, giving greater levels of responsibility to individuals and teams, distributing interesting work across various teams, setting targets which lead teams to a sense of achievement, and taking time to initiate and sustain positive interactions between team members;
- making very visible how the work of each individual member of staff and each team contributes value to the school;
- being aware of what demotivating factors seem to be in place at any given time and working to minimise their effect.

Strategic PIN down – Reflection 5.1	Aims
	◆ to consider personal experience of motivating and demotivating influences;
	◆ to apply the findings to a forthcoming team-based activity.

P – State the PROBLEM	A complicated, procedure dominated, mechanistic organisation demotivates. We must ...
I – Clarify the ISSUE	Since the main challenge of management in most organisations is to motivate and deal with people, the following golden rules should be observed ...
N – Tackle the NEED	The motivation of our staff is ... and requires...

This is a group exercise, though it can be carried out as individual reflection.

1   Number all participants 1, 2, 3, or 4. Give each participant one sheet off a flip chart. Ask all those with number 1 to think of a successful 'work-based' team situation which they have led, or in which they served as a member. Send them to do the following task on their flip sheet:

   a   describe in a telegraphic sentence the situation, team structure and task;

   b   list the ten most important 'motivators' which were in operation;

2   Give all number 3s the same task, but their scenario is to be an 'unsuccessful work-based team' and the 10 most significant demotivators.

3   Ask all 2s to do the same exercise as the 1s, but to choose a 'leisure-based team' Thus, successful leisure-based team and 10 most significant motivators.

4   All 4s do as 2s, but they concentrate on an unsuccessful leisure team situation and its 10 most demotivating influences.

5   After completion of this part of the exercise, display all flip sheets. Put motivators from both contexts on one wall or in one area, demotivators from both contexts in another location. Allow all participants time to review the lists and to clarify any uncertain descriptions. Then ask people to work in pairs and to summarise all of the lists by completing as much as they can of Table 5.1.

Strategic PIN down – Reflection 5.1 cont.

Table 5.1

	WORK motivators	LEISURE motivators
Atmosphere		
Actions		
Communications		
Incentives		
Methods		
Team characteristics		
	WORK demotivators	LEISURE demotivators
Atmosphere		
Actions		
Communication		
Incentives		
Methods		
Team characteristics		

6 Discuss the implications of the findings as follows:

◆ Our forthcoming team-based task is ...

◆ We should have in place these motivators ...

◆ We need to prevent these demotivators ... and minimise these ...

Issues in focus 5.3

The manner in which team leaders use the performance threshold standards may motivate or demotivate their colleagues. Heads of department, Key Stage co-ordinators, section leaders or pastoral leaders need to look for ways to use the initiative to strengthen collegiality. The final standard, which centres around effective professional characteristics, makes reference to 'inspiring trust and confidence' and 'building team commitment'. Team leaders are more likely to meet this standard if they do the following:

◆ use reciprocal lesson and school-based observations to build up a picture of the team's strengths and needs;

◆ take an active role in developing colleagues' professional capabilities;

◆ encourage shared thinking and development work concerning the team-specific implications of student performance data;

◆ take a lead in engaging the team in whole-school approaches to the curriculum, pupil management and effective provision to meet student diversity;

- show an interest in how members of the team are increasing their subject-specific or aspect-specific knowledge and understanding;
- involve the team in as many collaborative ventures as time and energy permits (for example, reviewing across the team the range of teaching styles and the types of learning in which students are engaged).

Team leaders can further review what they are doing already – and might do – by making reference to Hammond's (2000) multi-level matrix on using the threshold framework to improve team performance, and by considering the benefits of performance management as expressed by Forbat (2000).

5.3   Team cohesion

Terence

'There are as many opinions as there are people: each has his own correct way.'

Teams exist for many purposes. They may be put together on an *ad hoc* basis, they may be a group trained to a common standard and who comply with routines and procedures, even as far as wearing identical uniforms, they may be a self-managed unit, they may be 'think-tank' in style – that is a group of people deliberately brought together for conjecture and forward planning – they may be a group of volunteers who give of their time and energies out of interest in a particular endeavour, or in order to serve the community, they may come together because they share fundamental beliefs and therefore organise themselves into teams to consolidate those beliefs and spread their influence, they may function to achieve specific tasks under duress of time and risk (e.g. surgical teams, motor-racing pit teams, under-cover surveillance teams) or they may be loosely composed of people with different backgrounds and expertise who only function together as a team to fulfil a known remit within a defined period of time (for example, teams carrying out audit, inspection and market research).

In real life, few teams, whatever their purpose or composition, will be evenly balanced. It is not always possible to recruit or assign a perfect combination of talents, and even where this is principally achieved, the extent to which individuals are really committed or experienced team members will vary from person to person and group to group.

These circumstances mean that many teams have the properties of fluids. They may run one way, then another. They may flow easily around their tasks and environment, or be restricted or constricted by the internal difficulties they generate and the external barriers they encounter. They may remain as one unified movement and force, or intermittently break up into disconnected, smaller and less effective sub-systems. Teams are like this because:

◆ every member brings different capabilities and skills;
◆ in the initial stage of a project or exercise, each may hold different perspectives on the outcomes and how they should be achieved;
◆ members may experience tension between contributing to the team, securing its goals and doing other necessary work;
◆ the team's knowledge and expertise may be outstretched by the performance of other teams or by the demands of the task;
◆ they may be asked to deal with sensitive or controversial issues they did not have to face before;
◆ individuals may have less freedom of operation than they are used to in their more general role, especially with regard to making decisions and choosing the pattern of working;
◆ the team may be called upon to apply their thinking and skills under tight constraints of time and penalties for inappropriate outcomes.

However, though team roles, responsibilities, composition and working arrangements may be relatively fluid states, the responsibilities of a team leader are more consistent. Team leaders are the conduit through which the team:

◆ presents its identity, commitment and tone to the outside world;
◆ expresses its hopes and expectations;
◆ draws together its diversity to ensure reasonable consensus and actual results;
◆ maintains its structures and working practices;
◆ boosts its morale and commitment;
◆ passes on its frustrations and disagreements;
◆ reviews progress and plans future action.

Thus, a leader of a team undertakes a variety of roles. They act as:

◆ *motivator* – creating shared aspirations and commitment; bringing out the best that individuals can give; revitalising the team after a downturn; reshaping and redirecting the team when it needs to be reformed as key contributors leave, new blood arrives, or a different remit is presented; and, periodically, re-energising the team's action and commitment;

◆ *navigator* – clarifying the team's terms of reference and key objectives; maintaining a sense of progress if the route becomes obscured or the journey more severe or slower than expected; steering the introduction of new ideas; checking on progress and then renegotiating roles and tasks in order to complete the journey on time and to good effect;

◆ *co-ordinator* – co-ordinating the team's activities or monitoring such co-ordination; setting the team's work in the context of school policies; linking the team's work with that done by others; ensuring schedules, assignments, budgets and reviews are met; integrating multiple contributions and different types of information, and ensuring that the work of any sub-teams reconnects with the goals and tasks of the parent group;

◆ *evaluator* – checking that the work is being done in accordance with any 'code of conduct'; ensuring that the work is purposeful and to a high standard; monitoring that expected outcomes will be achieved on time and delivered in the manner expected; ensuring that the team's work complies with any required quality assurance arrangements, and checking and cross-checking the accuracy or quality of the evidence the team is using as the basis of its decisions and strategies.

Carrying out these roles does not have to be through the office of one person. If the team is experienced at the task, used to working together in constructive self-managed ways, has a variety of expertise and strengths, and is comfortable with the allocated procedures and working arrangements, the teamwork itself may be of sufficient harmony to ensure that flexible, interchangeable leadership occurs, or the team may act as a 'collective' needing only light steer from someone in the 'chair' role. This is more likely to be the case where teams are multi-skilled, comprised of members who are near equal in status, used to operating together for a significant period of time, and where the team shares a strong commitment to get the job done.

Many teams, however, including sometimes the most experienced, need to work on shaping a 'collective perspective'. That is a consensus perspective built from the members' disparate experiences, different viewpoints and the range of information and evidence they have to hand. Such a perspective is of particular value in education because the life and work of a school is dynamic, not static. Since it operates across a range of dimensions – managerial, organisational, pastoral and teaching – it is difficult for a single development agent or evaluator, no matter how professionally informed and talented, to capture an adequate picture of a school's vibrancy and justly pronounce upon it. A collective perspective is likely to be more representative of this variety and richness, and the school's strengths and areas for development. This is because a collective perspective offers the following advantages:

◆ sharing of ideas;
◆ balanced decision-making;
◆ judgements based on consensus;
◆ multiple viewpoints aid understanding of 'wholeness';
◆ wider sampling of opinions and experiences;
◆ questions/issues of significance addressed by the energy and skills of a team.

Issues in focus 5.4

Such corporate judgement is clearly expected within the inspection process, though is not as simple an affair as the following statement suggests:

'The sharing and testing of hypotheses and inspection issues will inform the corporate work of the team. The registered inspector should ensure that the overall judgements about the school command the agreement of the inspection team. These corporate judgements can most easily be reached through discussion involving all team members towards the end of the inspection. Ultimately the registered inspector must adjudicate, if necessary, and have the final word on judgements to be included in his or her report.'

Ofsted, 1995b, p. 33

Essentially, whatever role and responsibilities the team has, its task is to reach consensus. This process is easier if the team:

◆ has full awareness of its purpose and objectives;
◆ is clear about the issues on which it has to reach agreement;
◆ collects information and viewpoints in an agreed and systematic manner;
◆ understands the nature and strength of the information and data it collates and uses;

◆ knows where it stands on controversial issues;
◆ allows all members to speak and contribute;
◆ is made up of individuals who have the confidence to question judgements and decisions, and to seek clarification of that which they do not understand;
◆ has a process for airing and resolving disagreements;
◆ allows its members some time to think

The team will operate effectively if the leader or 'chair' does the following:

◆ provides relatively neutral handling of agenda items;
◆ keeps discussions on track so that contributions stay appropriate;
◆ gives direction during the discussion rather than strong opinion (perhaps by using Barker's (1993) six types of questions – closed, open, specific, overhead, relay and reverse);
◆ acts to provide summary statements and clarification of thinking at various points in the proceedings;
◆ highlights where the team agrees/disagrees/needs further discussion or more information;
◆ reminds the team of what they have to get across, to whom and by when;
◆ works to ensure that decisions are based on evidence and reasoned argument, not the 'power of clout and shout';
◆ resists the temptation to close too early by taking a vote.

Notice board 10 Some reasons why corporate judgements may not take place

◆ The promulgation of one person's thinking.

◆ Discussion/ meetings last too long.

◆ Task/focus/agenda is too sketchy.

◆ No one tackles the conflict or frustration.

◆ One member or a few dominate the event.

◆ Team is too big.

◆ Team is too small.

◆ No interim summaries.

◆ Some people are allowed to attend, yet contribute nothing.

◆ The Keep It Sweet and Simple (KISS) signpost is ignored.

◆ Irregular opportunities to work as a team and/ or team meetings too infrequent.

◆ Team believe they are tokenistic.

◆ Low morale and a lukewarm atmosphere.

◆ Nobody records the thinking or the decisions/proposals.

◆ The 'real' or important agenda is not on the table.

◆ Competition outstrips collaboration.

◆ The team has no real status or power.

◆ People are not kept to the point.

◆ Decision-making is all of one type.

Notice board 10 Some reasons why corporate judgements may not take place

- The chair or leader 'blames' at high volume, 'commends' at low.

- The group is at the 'storming' stage.

- Information presented to the team is too complex, too much, too disorganised.

- Timescale to explore thinking and reach agreement is inadequate.

- Team can't make the crucial or tough judgements unaided.

- Team wants too pure, too complete or too idealistic outcome.

- Discussion is too loose.

- Discussion is too formalised.

- No professional kudos or reward for completing the job.

- Too many members using the time to focus on other work – dealing with *their* agenda, not *the* agenda.

- Points of yield or compromise are passed.

- Team members are 'glued in', i.e. there by rank, tradition or patronage – not matched to needs of the task.

- The team is so mistrustful of each other that the only agenda item is 'passing the buck'.

Issues in focus 5.5

Most teams go through four distinct stages in their development (Tuckman 1965). These are cited in Field *et al.* (2000). They are:

Forming

At this stage the team is composed of individuals who will want to contribute to discussions about the team's purposes and at the same time will begin to *form* opinions about other members of the team, and particularly about the team leader. Some members will want to establish themselves in the team, by the nature and style of their contributions and by simple force of personality. The leader will be noting individual strengths, weaknesses and idiosyncrasies in readiness for the next stage of development.

Storming

Although there is consensus on the purposes of the team, some members may have been having second thoughts and may want to challenge the original purposes. As a result there may be *conflicts* and *hostilities* between some members of the team. Such conflicts are quite common and a natural part of team development, and it will be for the leader to handle these conflicts and differences in a balanced and sensitive way. The result is usually a set of revised purposes and early discussions on the ways the team can work to achieve the planned objectives.

$\downarrow$

Any revisions usually involve prioritising the purposes. Discussions are likely to centre around the balance of securing high-quality teaching, effective use of resources and improved standards of learning and achievement for all pupils. Team members can then begin to look at communication (informal and formal), planning (short-, medium and long-term) and decision-making (ways of contributing and influencing decisions).

Norming

The team begins to establish the ways it will work and how the objectives will be achieved. As these procedures become established, a sense of *team identity* begins to crystallise and members of the team feel free to discuss issues openly, and they begin to support each other. At this stage, purposes, objectives, responsibilities, provisional resource allocations, and procedures for monitoring and reviewing are recorded in draft written form.

Performing

There is a sense of *confidence and maturity* in the team, such that problems and issues are raised and discussed openly. Leaders will encourage members to reflect on their practices and regular reviews of objectives and the work of the team are considered normal.

It is valuable for all members of school staff to be aware of Tuckman's and other schemas which describe how teams develop. This enables them to feel more comfortable and assured at a particular stage, and by knowing the likely process of maturity, members can assist one another to progress more rapidly. These schemas also indicate that a 'task' cannot dominate teamworking in the absence of attention to the interpersonal dynamics.

Throughout the forming, storming, norming and performing stages, the leader might note Adair's three elements of effective leadership: namely, achieving the task, building and maintaining the team, and developing the individual. The leader has to balance all three elements in order to achieve the team's purposes and objectives (Adair, 1986)

Strategic PIN down – Reflection 5.2	**Aims**

◆ to examine one simple procedure for resolving differences in the course of shaping a collective perspective;

◆ to improve on it for use in one's own work context.

P – State the PROBLEM	As far as possible, disagreement has to be turned into agreement because ...
I – Clarify the ISSUE	Giving direction without domination means ...
N – Tackle the NEED	Our people will more easily reach agreement if ...

If marked differences arise within a team as it tackles a task or agenda, it is helpful to adopt a systematic approach to resolution, since this may prevent the team from agonising without focus, or spending time drifting endlessly across an ocean of disparate pieces of information and disconnected ideas.

Consider the following structure:

1 Spotlight What is the issue?
Clarification may be an important contribution towards resolution. It is easy to lose sight of focus and possibilities in the plethora of activities and information which make up the daily business of schools and teamwork.

2 Diagnosis What is the difficulty?
Is it lack of information, lack of evidence, contrary opinions, grievance, or something else?

3 Investigation
What manageable aspects of the issue can be used to focus energy and discussion?

4 Sort
Seek views on the best course of action. Key questions are – what results/outcomes do we want from our discussion / efforts? Is there only one course of action or can we present a range of alternatives? If helpful, arrange at this stage for additional information and/or second opinions. List all the possibilities.

Strategic PIN down – Reflection 5.2 cont.

5 Get 'best fit'
Confirm the majority view. Indicate how far it represents the perspective of everyone. Describe it fully for all concerned. Record it as a tentative course of action. Link it to a proposed timeline.

6 Implement
Put in place the decision or proposed action.

7 Review
Return to issue and see if consensus or a majority view still holds and/or has improved / decreased in strength. If necessary, return to step one.

Develop this approach so that it has more relevance for your context. Consider more information / more questions at each stage; more stages; making a diagrammatic version of the structure; comparing it with another system, then choosing the best from both; using it to build a better framework.

5.4 Conflict resolution

Anonymous

'ANGER is only one letter short of DANGER.'

People divide sharply and sometimes bitterly over the description 'conflict resolution'. Those against the term and the ideas behind it suggest that in accepting the notion of conflict, one is setting the mind away from more positive orientations such as the idea of the 'win-win solution' (O'Brien, 1993). Others see conflict as a manifestation of complex crisis, or a type of unwanted behaviour, for which there are teachable handling and coping skills (Honey, 1980; Parry, 1990; Everard and Morris,1990).

Schmuck *et al.* (1972) suggest that few schools will not have degrees of conflict given that they are complex organisations with their own intricate dynamics:

'Conflicts are ubiquitous in complex organisations, the best strategy for dealing with them differs from case to case. The most effective strategy depends on the severity of the disagreement, who the adversaries are, whether the conflict is potentially constructive (i.e. will produce creative tensions) or destructive, and on the authority, resources, and knowledge the administrator or teacher possesses.'

p.136

Others argue that, since in most organisations demands are complex, interrelated and need simultaneous handling, one might expect more conflict scenarios than seem to be the case. There is a suggestion in this line of reasoning that calling up inappropriate actions or behaviour, or confronting an individual or group, is often avoided until it escalates into direct conflict or it damages the image and efficiency of the workplace.

> 'One of the biggest problems facing American management is the unwillingness to confront problem behaviour. We tend to promote, transfer, reorganize around, and cater to problem employees. Where is the ability to step up to the problem of confronting the way employees behave while they do their jobs? Is it no longer within the realm of the manager's ability to influence the company culture? We predict that today and tomorrow's manager must be excellent at reading behaviour, interpreting it, rewarding and disciplining it. It will no longer be good enough to be a good manager of paper. Managing people is far more complex than just assigning them work.'
>
> Barr and Barr, 1989, p. 166

A counter-view to this is that some leaders and managers may fuel the potential for conflict by their attitude, bullishness, ineptitude or overt unfairness. For example, when the TUC set up their 'bad boss' hotline they had 5,000 calls in one week. If only a small percentage of these were regarded as of real concern, there is no room for complacency regarding manager–employee relations. Indeed, all of the three positions outlined – that is, conflict almost inevitable in complex organisations, managers not tackling troublesome behaviour until it has sown the seeds of, or caused conflict, and managers contributing to conflict by the way in which they exercise their role – indicate that whatever approach is taken to its resolution:

> 'In order to give a complete and relatively realistic account of organisation working, we need to acknowledge the possibilities of conflict and offer sources of advice.'
>
> Fidler, 1996, p. 81

In recent research about effective school leadership, Lawlor and Sills (2000) found that one of the most difficult and challenging situations for headteachers was handling staff conflict. The initial findings from the study showed that effective headteachers tackle difficult staff situations head on, while being careful to carry as many colleagues as possible along with the decision, base any decisions on the evidence available, and carefully follow all personnel procedures.

In making a judgement about what sources of advice to offer, it may be helpful to put the wide-ranging and complex concept of conflict into some kind of pragmatic framework. This outcome can be arrived at by means of the PACT system – People, Action, Communication and Text. It may be helpful to develop a file or folder system of ideas and information around this framework. The acronym is a useful reminder that, at the end of the day, serious disagreements or conflicts are only resolved by negotiation and agreement between two or more parties.

5.4.1 People

◆ Take the best advice available from the assertiveness movement. In particular, learn to recognise different types of assertive behaviour in self and others and consider various ways of handling such behaviour.

◆ As far as possible seek to empathise rather than earmark. That is, develop techniques of active listening, neutral chairing and boundary setting, since these techniques allow intervention, while lessening the risk of getting too deeply involved in the emotions and temperament being shown.

◆ Separate out the 'signal' from the surrounding 'noise'. Deal with the message while doing all that is reasonable to ignore or play down the 'heat' of its delivery.

◆ Seek to distinguish between actions which may be reasonable 'creative tension' during the development of a project or a pressurised part of the academic year, and behavioural or other incidents which if over-trivialised could lead to more serious conflict. For example, some teams generate high degrees of steam in coming to a decision or strategy, but this does not necessarily lead to impaired working relationships. In contrast, mild – but intentional harassment – tends to get worse if left unchecked. Stay close to the idea that it is best to tackle symptoms early, because they are signals to later impending disaster.

5.4.2 Action

◆ Decide as quickly as possible what is the nature of the conflict – for example, disagreement about strategic objectives, working practices, staff deployment, pupil management, or the accessibility, allocation and use of resources. Concisely explain the interpretation made for the benefit of others. Don't assume that in the heat of the moment they recognise the full nature of the disagreement.

◆ As with the identification of pupil problem behaviour, try to avoid describing the nature of the conflict in very general, exalted and non-specific terms. Don't be tempted to elevate it by surrounding it in topical 'management speak' – instead, seek to analyse the nature of the decisions or the people problems which are its base.

◆ In respect of the latter, consider carefully any 'pay-offs' which may be operating for teams or individuals, and then look to ways of reducing such rewards. For example, Honey (1980) describes pay-offs for the 'negative man' (though the pay-offs may relate equally to either sex):

- *'on a high percentage of occasions resistance wins the day;*
- *proposers pay attention to him;*
- *people congratulate him for being a stickler;*
- *he avoids having to change anything or at least minimises the things he has to change;*
- *he gets himself into a position where he can say "If things go wrong, don't blame me. I warned you";*
- *his subordinates show they admire the way he protects/ represents their interests.'*

◆ Try to ensure that those most affected by the situation play a key role in the analysis of the conflict, the search for resolutions, and the ultimate decision on which strategies to try. Summarise everybody's agreement before closing the matter.

5.4.3 Communication

◆ Ensure that all oral and written communication relating to a conflict situation is clear and concise.

◆ Try to keep communication in the 'blameless mode' – that is, focused, practical and neutral, rather than emotive, lofty and threatening.

◆ Allow easy access to any written communications (policies, handbook guidance, etc.) which reinforces how people are expected to proceed and behave if conflict or grievance arises.

5.4.4 Text

◆ Develop a personal reminder card on how best to deal with and resolve conflicts. Carry it with you or review it from time to time. It is better to occasionally think through the issue and be well informed about advice and strategies, than to be seeking 'in the head for such advice' in the middle of a difficult and possibly fraught situation.

◆ Have a clear and readily accessible policy on conflict and possible procedures for its resolution, but frame this policy on guidelines which may prevent it – for example, pragmatic advice on equal opportunities and the avoidance of bullying and harassment.

◆ Keep a detailed log on any incident of bullying, harassment or incitement aimed at self or others. Make sure the log contains any relevant evidence. The log may reflect a pattern which calls for a whole school review. The information will also be essential if it is necessary to begin a grievance procedure.

◆ Maintain an e-mail list or general directory of people or organisations outside the school who may need to be contacted swiftly for advice or help.

◆ Organise this information tidily, concentrating on ease of access and use; use any guidelines on managing conflict and any relevant tribunal information issued by DfEE, LEAs and national organisations.

5.5 Stress management

Swedish proverb

'Worry often gives a small thing a big shadow.'

It is now generally agreed that stress may have positive as well as negative features. There are many situations – for example, being interviewed, making a presentation to a large audience, or leading an important meeting – when to be 'keyed up' to a reasonable level is likely to lead to a better performance than remaining in a state in which one exhibits too little zeal, or is rather too laid back. On another plane, some people deliberately seek environmental or emotionally stressful situations for cathartic purposes. They may engage in physically dangerous exploits, group dynamic encounters, or mind baffling games because they believe that the experience – though it may give them degrees of stress during the 'doing' phase – is in the longer term a positive exposure of self-to-self, an opportunity to face a testing situation and to emerge the better for it.

Some experts, however, argue that it is more sensible to identify these facets of challenge as 'states of arousal', thereby reserving the term 'stress' for those physical and emotional reactions which indicate that a person is at a point near to collapse, or beyond functioning in a way that is stable and constructive for themselves and others.

'Stress has become part of common parlance in that it is used to describe a range of feelings. Young people and adults talk of being 'stressed' on a regular basis. This recognises that life has changed and that pressure and stress are more common than they were. However, it also devalues the experience, in that those who are experiencing stress find it harder to accept this as a genuinely difficult experience, for

everyone is using the word to describe experiences ranging from temporary dissatisfaction on a "bad" day to feelings of pressure. It makes it harder to take seriously our own feelings and experiences of stress.'

McLaughlin, 1997, p. 164

More recent thinking also suggests that in an environment of uncertainty, such as this competitive and problem-dominated world, being stressed is inevitable for everyone at some points in their lives. Stress is seen as standing in a relationship to human endeavour, akin to that of the geographical interface between sea to land. One can understand the composition of the sea, learn to navigate it, find safe harbours in times of tempests, know one's personal reaction to states of the sea and how best to respond, protect others from the vagaries of the sea, or rescue compatriots from its most volatile states – but in no sense is it possible to completely control the sea. Stress, perhaps, is like the fluidity of the sea – a current that can be utilised purposefully, given the right preparation and the appropriate human equipment, but ever present and capable of wreaking great havoc and destruction, especially if safe measures are ignored, or it is approached in too cavalier a fashion when at its most turbulent.

Using a different analogy, one might describe stress as something like the universe. There is an integration of sorts to the universe and it has many discernible elements and patterns. But its overall presence is too vast, too varied and too rich to be understood in simple terms. We can understand the principles of the universe, trace some of its existing patterns and have some idea of its overall make-up, but the bigger picture is not static like that of a jigsaw, it is an ever changing state of affairs.

If correct, such views of stress suggest that its management demands something more than a simple first aid kit of techniques to apply when facing stress provoking situations or their aftermath. A better approach is to understand what one can from the complex dynamic that stress is, and work with it, instead of seeing it as a tangible state or set of circumstances which can be instrumentally managed and controlled.

What, then, do we know of the 'bigger picture' we call stress?

◆ Potentially stressing situations permeate human life and endeavour as completely as gases pervade the atmosphere. These gases, when in balance, aid the living process, but their pressure, movement and contribution to combustion can threaten or destroy the very same process. So with stress. Degrees of it may motivate, strengthen resolve, lead to sensible preparation to meet the challenge and result in an effective performance, the discharge of which results in a feeling of stress reduction. Conversely, if degrees of it are perceived to be too burdensome, one may avoid stress by opting out of situations thought not to be manageable, or the exposure to stress-provoking situations may become so overwhelming that they lead to distorted reactions and eventual breakdown or death. As with other types of pressure, it is the extremes which cause problems.

◆ Most, if not all stress, is both mental and physical. Physical damage or fatigue can induce states of confusion and anxiety leading to stress, and the power of the mind to allow us to be anxious, alarmist, aggressive and angry can lead to bodily effects which in themselves are stressful.

◆ Some stress can arise from a mismatch between basic human traits and the working, domestic or life circumstances prevailing for each person at a given moment in time. For example, a need to get on with the job and produce something perceived as tangible and worthwhile, may be arrested if working for an organisation which is severely constrained politically, or whose pace towards the eventual goal or product is slowed down by drawn-out procedures and long-winded working practices. These conflicting circumstances – individual predisposition versus circumstantial constraints – can create significant internal stress for the person involved.

◆ Though it may be relatively straightforward to recognise signs of stress, it is not always easy to distinguish between cause and effect. Stress reactions may be carried into the current situation from more distant work, domestic or social events; be created within the context as the individual's inner perceptions or turmoil collide with the demands of a specific task or challenge; or be a 'flashpoint response' to shifts in pressure levels which are the consequence of a number of competing influences that have been building up for some time. Equally, stress reactions may develop because the individual or team has no strategy or training to deal with particular situations, which if inadequately handled over a period of time, may lead to them feeling stressed. Examples of situations with this potential include ineffective interpersonal relationships, immature parenting skills, poor time or project management, feeling insecure in a team which is not focused and managed, or working on a project where management responsibility for the outcomes changes hands frequently.

◆ Each individual's capacity to handle pressure will vary with their age, the state of their health, their general level of motivation for life, and their capability to handle major events occurring in their work, social relationships, general life and family circumstances. Major life changes such as a serious accident to self or a loved one, bereavement, changing job, marriage, divorce, having children, moving to a new location to live or work, losing a long-standing job, and suffering a profound loss in personal skills or status have the potential to set up stress reactions and trigger temporary or more sustained breakdown.

◆ The effects of being in a stress-related state can include biological responses, such as nausea, heart attack, significant twitching or insomnia; impaired professional judgements; fatal errors; damaged work or domestic relationships; increased proneness to states of illness; temper outbursts or periods of confusion; a tendency to self-abuse (including working excessive hours); drinking too much alcohol; restarting or increasing smoking, and denigrating oneself to a point of total despair.

So how do all these facets of stress relate to education leadership? First, whether leadership is an individual or collective responsibility, those 'in-charge' need to have some knowledge of the 'big picture' of stress and to accept the moral and professional responsibility to reduce situations which can initiate or accentuate stress reactions. Such situations include:

◆ leaving people in prolonged states of insecurity, uncertainty, powerlessness or danger;
◆ introducing new expectations, new directions or new challenges without informing others on reasons why, and then failing to prepare those who have to make the changes;
◆ failing to provide reassurance, encouragement and support at times of great pressure or when major changes or upheavals occur;
◆ allowing an individual or group under stress to put too much pressure on other individuals or another group;
◆ downsizing, asset stripping or risk taking, to a point where it is no longer possible for a team to meet its objectives and still maintain a balance between effort and rest;
◆ reflecting a view on any individual or team in trouble, that it is the result of 'wimpish' behaviour or inadequate personal characteristics, rather than professional shortcomings or professional circumstances.

Second, realising that, in the absence of self-referral by an individual or team, there are no specific symptoms which unequivocally indicate a significant stress reaction. There are diagnostic indicators which may suggest a need for action or support, but these may arise from other circumstances than feeling stressed. Thus, diagnostic indicators are best regarded as tentative hypotheses to be cross-checked with trusted viewpoints or other information, including self-reporting by individuals or teams, if the latter testimony can be regarded as valid at the time.

Indicators which may be significant are:

◆ a marked change in *behaviour* (conscientious and punctilious, to erratic and indifferent; relaxed and reasonably carefree, to ritualistic and obsessional; steady and reliable to increased nervousness; tidy and well turned out, to becoming unkempt):
◆ prolonged and severe *mood changes* (loss of an outward-going nature; loss of humour; increased and sustained levels of anxiety, not previously present; acute anxiety about a specific job or task, well beyond the level of tension it may demand; increased agitation, or altered patterns of thinking);
◆ *changed physical responses* (increased indigestion or nausea; a marked increase in tiredness which is not obviously related to some temporary cause; tremors, fainting or palpitation; general fatigue; a move to being irrational about personal health matters);
◆ alteration in the *expression of feelings* (moving to a state of being over-controlling; too compliant and conforming; perhaps 'stewing' rather than expressing an opinion or taking a decisive action; becoming more angry, tearful and cynical).

Third, leadership is unlikely to be that of managing a diagnosis or managing the symptoms. It will centre more around assisting the individual or team to regain a balanced composure or state of confidence. It will involve putting into place strategies or systems which will alleviate the symptoms of stress, or more valuably, seeking ways to reduce the risk of their occurrence. Leadership also has a role in ensuring there are guidelines on how to respond to stress which may have reached crisis point and when and how to refer to medical or other specialist advice.

Issues in focus 5.6

Some years ago, the Manchester Institute of Science and Technology drew up an occupational 'stress league' for the *Sunday Times*. Teachers did not feature in the top twenty ratings. That position is unlikely to be the case today. Recent research findings, union surveys, LEA data, the focus of some regional and local ↓

INSET courses, and newspaper fact finding and case studies, all point to teachers feeling more stressed now than at any other time in the history of state-funded education. This is also confirmed by a survey from the helpline 'Teacherline'. An examination of its data has revealed an estimated 200,000 calls over the past two years, with 'workload' given as the primary reason for seeking help (*Guardian* report – 22 May 2000).

Though the pressure of inspection did contribute to a teacher's suicide as early as 1888 (see page 28), more recent tragic deaths in which inspection and the pressures of work appear to be contributing factors, once again highlight growing teacher unhappiness with balancing the requirements of the job with central demands for greater accountability and higher across-the-board standards of student achievement. Clearly, not all teachers think they are 'stressed out' and the degree of stress perceived and experienced varies considerably depending on the size and type of school, the quality of the management, the geographical and socio-economic area the school serves, its 'history' through recent Ofsted inspections, and the amount and type of support it can call forth from volunteers, the LEA, governors and parents. However, in general, teachers continue to talk of low morale and increased stress, and the contributory factors are widespread. They include:

◆ perceived loss of status due to successive governments and the media 'naming and shaming' and generally maintaining a poor press for teachers;
◆ direct criticism of teaching methods;
◆ grading of teachers by inspectors;
◆ the general range and depth of large-scale changes to education introduced in the 1988–98 period, and continuing to some extent today;
◆ more students with low morale, difficult behaviour and troublesome home circumstances;
◆ teachers, like others, affected by the tensions inherent in a society more openly litigious;
◆ generally longer working hours;
◆ more systems of accountability, more frequently applied;
◆ limited job security and promotion prospects;
◆ diminished union power and negotiating rights;
◆ a general intensification of demand in all aspects of professional work – teaching (including the revisions to the National Curriculum); student management and welfare; assessment, recording and reporting; and whole school demands, including in some schools giving time to aspects of classroom and school maintenance;
◆ in general, an increased atmosphere of uncertainty and fear.

Though there is some evidence that the worst excesses of control and change are now over, as yet there is no major upbeat in teacher morale. Recruitment to the profession is requiring additional incentives in some subjects, and how teachers will respond to new performance management structures and revised arrangements for their continuing professional development remains to be seen. The continuing state of flux and the developing and widespread demands on teachers suggest that leaders need to recognise more strongly the potential the profession now has for stress-induced burnout. Responses to stress need to:

◆ be across the board and at many different levels (individual, team, school and self);
◆ distinguish between role-related, team-related, person-centred and school-based stress;
◆ include for each school an audit of what practical things are possible;
◆ create a climate where asking for professional ideas and help is the norm;
◆ contribute periodic advice on stress management as part of the school's INSET programme;
◆ ensure the planning of back-up training and maintenance schedules for all new technology and other machinery which has the power to severely disrupt targets and deadlines;
◆ approach individual and teacher accountability with good sense and minimalist extra work;
◆ ensure that teacher (and leaders') targets for professional and career advancement are realistic;
◆ make time in meetings and other events for recharging the team spirit;
◆ attempt to tackle student as well as teacher stress;
◆ offer access to a library of useful advice. McLaughlin (1997) offers a brief but very practical overview of stress factors; Cox *et al.* (1989) take a problem-solving approach; Brown (1999) provides a thorough educational perspective on the emotional issues of loss, change and grief, and Cooper (1995) covers stress in the workplace.

Finally, the essential aim is to *prevent* stress rather than have to manage the consequences. The education leader's role is similar to that now asked of medical professionals – that is, to apply knowledge and skills towards developing and implementing programmes of physical and psychological health and well-being, in preference to working only with the consequences of poor body management, physical disease and nervous breakdown.

Strategic PIN down – Reflection 5.3	**Aims**

♦ to explore positive responses to controlling work stress;
♦ to start to create a set of guidelines aimed at preventing stress before it occurs.

P – State the PROBLEM   Given that the causes of stress are diverse and many-sided ...

I – Clarify the ISSUE   No one is immune from the effects of stress. This means that the basis of managing stress needs ...

N – Tackle the NEED   General personal make-up and previous experience can lead to stress influences being very individual ...

Task

Modify and supplement the following statements to create a set of useful guidelines,

Physical

♦ Audit the school's physical environments for any sources of stress and modify those features which can be altered.
♦ Check out noise, ventilation and lighting to see if reduction or modification is necessary.
♦ Do teachers and students have sufficient space to work comfortably? If not, what modifications can be made?
♦ Can students' work be used in a manner which helps to create a relaxing ambience?
♦ Offer opportunities to staff and students to learn easily applied relaxation techniques or provide information about them.
♦ Encourage participation in fun-type physical exercise.
♦ Give clear advice on and training in how to use any technical equipment (e.g. ICT and reprographics) which may cause discomfort or stress if used inappropriately.

Psychological

♦ Talk about and recognise stress as a pervasive set of circumstances. Does everyone know their own 'pressure gauge'? Can they distinguish between pressure and stress?
♦ Lead by example regarding proper access to rest and recreational time. Encourage maximum use of daily break times, non-contact time, flexible working, and leave periods.

Strategic PIN down – Reflection 5.3 cont.	◆ Don't make working long hours a virtue or part of the culture.
	◆ Modify any 'systems failures' which may be lowering self-esteem such as ineffective communications; inefficient procedures; unvarying routines (e.g. staff meetings) which lead to disinterest in the nature of the work and the quality of outcomes; maintaining inappropriate timetables or work schedules which result in, or run the risk of, consistent mental and physical deterioration, etc.
	◆ When change is necessary prepare for it, persuade others of its value, phase it in as much as possible, allow time for people to adapt; be encouraging and supportive, even if former efficiency levels dip at first.
	◆ If colleagues seek medical or other help to manage stress – offer what temporary relief it is possible to arrange within the school without loss of benefit to students and loss of face for the individual.

5.6 Summary

'The creative environment is not always comfortable. For comfort join a club. To organise for creativity, prepare for life without certainty. You enjoy less order, you institutionalise more uncertainty, you share leadership, you run what others see as an untidy ship, and to top it all, you have no guarantee of success. Its absence, however, does in time guarantee failure.'

Terry O'Connor

- ◆ A climate which encourages leadership by all grows from attention to team motivation, team coherence and team strengths, coupled with attention to and strategies for conflict resolution and the management of stress.
- ◆ Individuals and teams display subtle differences. There is no definite or single set of rules which guarantees their motivation and commitment.
- ◆ High morale, together with the will to achieve goals, are the centre pieces of team motivation. A team leader needs to demonstrate care, as well as show confidence, commitment and creativity.
- ◆ Leadership roles can be shared across experienced teams. This does not preclude the need for the headteacher to exercise governance over the work of individual teachers and teams of staff.
- ◆ The use of collective responsibility is becoming an accepted feature of effective management and focused professional development. Teachers must be encouraged to share collective responsibility and the building up of corporate judgements.

◆ Stress is present in everyday life and only becomes a problem when it exceeds the individual's or team's capacity to live and respond positively and effectively.

◆ Stress leads to both mental and physical reactions because of the interconnections between mind and body.

◆ Since leaders are often change agents, part of a system or set of challenges which may involve prolonged exposure to changing circumstances, or the instigators of different working arrangements or altered physical conditions, they need to understand the 'big picture' of stress, how to alleviate it and how to reduce the risk of stress reaching crisis point.

◆ It is necessary to manage one's own stress to help others with theirs.

Chapter 6 — Leadership as a catalyst for creativity

6.1 Overview

In Chapter 1 we briefly outlined features of social and technological change and their relationship with professional standards and the school as a learning and developing organisation. Chapter 2 questioned the overall efficacy of individualism and presented educational leadership in preference to just 'leader'. By examining some whole school issues in Chapter 3, we hoped to show that school improvement is a team effort requiring the on-going development of professional capabilities across the board. Chapters 4 and 5 further shaped this view by reference to the importance of corporate actions, including collective decision-making and a team response to sustaining motivation and minimising professional stress. It is time now to look at leadership as a catalyst for creativity. By this we mean engaging commitment, energising the change process, encouraging cross-disciplinary teamwork, and nurturing school-based action research. Energetic and imaginative approaches to these areas of professionalism result in schools with a distinctive brand of creativity and confidence.

6.2 Engaging commitment

> 'Never doubt that a small group of thoughtful, committed people can change the world; indeed it's the only thing that ever has.'
>
> Margaret Meade

Because of journalistic and popular interest in 'conviction' as the end product or not of a criminal trial, this term is not much used in professional language these days. This is a pity, since the word in its major referent sense and in its older meaning, indicates the state of *being convinced* or pursuing a *firmly held belief* to some point of effect. As Margaret Meade's statement above implies, *conviction underpins commitment*. It is only when people are truly convinced about a particular need or a specific course of action that they become really committed to meeting the need or taking the action. This is as true of students as adults. Everyone knows that it is not really 'desk time' that establishes learner confidence and performance, but the interaction of a shared conviction between teacher and student about the value of what is being studied and how it is being learned. In particular, when students are convinced that what they learn in school will make a real difference to their chances in life and to their enjoyment of life, they become committed to the achievement of learning goals.

Though most sustained strategic and operational success within schools, sections and teams is seldom due solely to the charisma and guidance of one individual, an innovator with an imaginative idea can make a big difference as to how the future is positively visualised and planned for. Strong and creative leadership by an individual, when coupled with drive and determination, often produces a sense of conviction and mission which makes others feel that strategy is directed towards a defined and worthwhile end. No leader will inspire colleagues to plan and join a journey, in anything but a 'going through the motions' manner if they see that leader as lacking in resolution about purpose and commitment.

In this sense, for all leaders and for all groups, commitment is not far removed from intense conviction and dedication. It is a deep seated will to achieve a goal, to cause a change or to make a difference. Inspiring by example, by demonstrating positive thinking, by showing determination to a cause, and by staying with a 'long haul' are features of commitment to which others most readily respond. The full range of the actual qualities that constitute commitment by an individual or team may not always be overt to an interested observer, but they are 'obvious' to those so influenced.

'Although the leaders themselves don't mention it, those who like and respect their leaders talk of their "idealism", their "integrity", the "trust she puts in you and you respond", their sense of humour ... their ability to convince ... of the confident pride in all that the school community achieves, together with its restless determination and expectation to achieve more, rather than sit back on its laurels...

Brighouse and
Woods, 1999
Especially convincing to staff is commitment, evidenced by time and energy given to the task.'

Issues in focus 6.1

The research by Lawlor and Sills (1999) into the characteristics of effective headteachers identified fourteen attributes:

1   the ability to work simultaneously on a variety of issues and problems;
2   has clear, shared values and vision;
3   passion for students' development and achievement;
4   understands the need for, and practises, well-developed interpersonal skills;
5   sets high expectations;
6   uses monitoring and evaluation for improvement;
7   prepared to take risks;
8   high levels of knowledge, understanding and professional confidence;
9   appropriate use of structures and systems;
10 efficient use of time;
11 political awareness and skills;
12   integrated approach to strategic and operational issues;
13 whole school perspective and approach;
14 positive commitment to staff development.

In addition, personal qualities and attributes emerged as crucial and permeated the whole range of headteachers' interventions. These included the following characteristics of highly effective leadership identified by the headteachers themselves:

◆   the passion and commitment to help pupils make progress and to raise achievement;
◆   high expectations of staff and students and the use of evidence to challenge students and staff as a means of changing behaviour;
◆   motivating, valuing, challenging and trusting staff, and getting the different relationships right;
◆   risk-taking as part of a climate of trust;
◆   high levels of professional knowledge, understanding and confidence;
◆   effective communication encompassing openness, consulting and listening;
◆   highly developed personal qualities, not least a sense of humour putting people at their ease, and a strong presence that inspires continuing confidence among all stakeholders.

It is clear from the observations of Brighouse and Woods, from day-to-day experience, from the Lawlor and Sills' (1999) findings, and from other research evidence, that people are galvanised around behaviours which say 'I believe in what I say'. But such 'self-identifying' behaviour is more complex than it looks. When successful it is linked with reassurance to others about commitment. This arises from the following:

◆ some faith by staff in those who 'say they are committed';
◆ some actions that demonstrate that such faith is not misplaced;
◆ some demonstration by the leadership of a genuine belief that the school is there to 'make a difference' and not there merely to contain students;
◆ some clarity about the educational values 'we go to the stake' for;
◆ some understanding that 'quality' or 'excellence' has been adequately contextualised and the commitment is aligned with a manageable and reachable goal;
◆ some evidence that the 'objective', 'task' or 'project' is taken seriously and is not simply 'flavour of the month', an initiative for its own sake, or an action because 'we need to be seen to be doing something';
◆ some determination to justify and obtain the necessary time and resources to lift the initiative off the launch pad and to place it securely within an appropriate trajectory or orbit.

In short, the work being done, and that which it is intended will be done, have to be seen to be meaningful, to fully engage the leadership as well as the team, to be achievable, and to be directed at targets which will make an important contribution to students' capabilities and their general well-being. When these factors are at the right intermix, school morale is usually high, teacher attitudes are positive and teachers' commitment beneficially focused. However, securing the proper mix involves society in general, as well as school leadership. This is because vigorous and sustained commitment correlates with various types of trust. According to Ford (1995), these are:

◆ management's trust in their employees' competence;
◆ management's trust in their employees' motives;
◆ employees' trust in management's competence;
◆ employees' trust in management's motives.

Regular visits to schools, to teacher INSET, and to professional forums of various kinds, suggests that much has yet to be done to bring these four states into being, especially when for the latter two, management is writ large to include the Government, DfEE and LEAs, as well as school leadership at the level of the individual institution. There is still a good deal of mistrust permeating these interfaces and an atmosphere of mutual respect is not yet secure. That it needs to be is all too apparent at the common-sense level, but also because research shows that:

> *'schools with committed, satisfied teachers have less teacher absenteeism, lower turnover, less burnout and less dysfunctional classroom behaviour ... and teachers have a sense of efficacy about their work ... but in contrast ... teachers with a high sense of academic futility were less likely to push their pupils to do well ... felt there was little they could do to ensure that all pupils achieve at a high level ... and for them, the custodial function of schooling outweighed the educative.'*

Willms, summarising various research findings, 1992, p. 76

Given that commitment and morale are also a feature of accepting the appropriateness of the school's goals and values, all staff must be encouraged to participate in decision-making about the school's primary mission and its short-term and long-term objectives. Inevitably, both types of objectives will point to degrees of change and in order to underpin and sustain commitment, it is important to identify at the individual, team and school levels what is the 'present' position and what is the 'better' position, i.e. that after the proposed change. Formalising an agreed mission statement may be a helpful process and setting in place some success indicators (e.g. in x time y will be achieved to z level) can help people's determination to keep on track. However, as mentioned earlier, the range and quality of collegial decision-making is a prime contributor to commitment and morale. Not least, because we make time for, and give effort to, those things in which we believe and in which we have a primary stake.

However, commitment like motivation is not a once attained, then statically held state. Indeed, the biggest challenge to any individual leader or leadership team, as for any teacher in relation to their classes and their students, is the maintenance of morale and commitment. Evangelising on its own will have little effect. Actions and progress have to be presented not in promissory note form, but as a true 'working towards' record. In particular good commitment has to be:

◆ reinforced all the time;
◆ supported regularly by those in charge;
◆ centred on a common and purposeful goal;
◆ linked to what benefits are happening and why they are happening;

◆ maintained through regular school activities that facilitate participation and co-operation;

◆ sustained by intrinsic and extrinsic rewards.

As with some aspects of students' behaviour, good team commitment is usually sustained by recognising and highlighting the positive. Strategies might include:

◆ giving genuine compliments for work completed;

◆ showing pride in the team;

◆ providing individuals with a written description of something unique they contribute to the team;

◆ showing how the team contributes to the school's synergy (how it contributes to a level of effectiveness which is greater than the sum of the parts);

◆ explaining how the work of the team is helping the school to meet specific objectives;

◆ profiling the team's achievements with governors, parents, external support staff and other relevant agencies;

◆ offering further responsibilities;

◆ seeking their advice on curriculum and professional matters;

◆ drawing out how their attitudes, skills and technical capabilities equip them for a more demanding job in hand;

◆ reviewing how they have met (are meeting) certain performance standards;

◆ asking what can be done to help the team develop its own growth and professionalism;

◆ boosting positive thinking by the judicious use of well chosen 'action statements' (see Notice board 11).

Notice board 11 Some inspiring action statements

◆ Keep your ideals high enough to inspire you and low enough to encourage you.

◆ It's better to furnish the future than varnish the past.

◆ If you want to defend an objective, practice it.

◆ Make sure your intentions are not just pretensions.

◆ A person's work is a self-portrait.

◆ No one ever fails until they fail inside.

◆ Doing beats stewing

◆ Every accomplishment, great or small, starts with the words – 'I'll try.'

◆ Begin where you are but don't stay where you are. ↓

> **Notice board 11 Some inspiring action statements cont.**
>
> ◆ Think of a doubt as an invitation to think.
>
> ◆ Life's heaviest burden is to have nothing to carry.
>
> ◆ If you don't stand for something you will likely fall for anything.
>
> ◆ Choice, not chance, determines destiny.
>
> ◆ There's always a good crop of food for thought. What is needed is enough enthusiasm to harvest it.
>
> ◆ An error does not become a mistake until you refuse to correct it.

Strategic PIN down – Reflection 6.1

Aims

◆ to use the word 'commitment' to develop a checklist of characteristics which sustain it;

◆ to review a team's commitment in the light of these characteristics.

Complete the second column in Table 6.1 and rate the strength for a specified team

Team: ....

Rating scale: ....

1 = Strong 2 = Adequate 3 = Needs some development 4 = Needs urgent attention

Table 6.1

Characteristic	Strength for team
C	
O	
M	
M	
I	
T	
M	
E	
N	
T	

For any 4s - set down the direction in which change is needed and what might achieve the change. For example:

Change needed   What might achieve the change?
Reduce tension and grievances

Having completed this exercise it might be valuable to explore where this team stands on the 'team performance curve' as described by Katzenbach and Smith (1993).

Issues in focus 6.2

Katzenbach and Smith (1993) define a team as a *small number of people with complementary skills* who are *committed to a common purpose, performance goals, and approach* for which they hold themselves *mutually accountable*. They outline a sequence of team development. Through appropriate opportunities and successes, a high performance team arises as follows:

- working group – lacks a significant performance need; this is essential to the formation of a team;
- pseudo team – a team in name only. No specific performance need, because no focus on a collective challenge or no record of collective achievement;
- potential team – definite or significant performance need, but not yet harmonising to the point of effective impact;
- team – focused, purposeful, collective perspective and actions, acceptance of accountability;
- high performance team – a team with 'plus factors', including members who are deeply committed to the team and to each other's personal growth and success.

6.3 Energising the change process

'Learning usually passes through three stages. First, we know the right answers. Second, we learn the right questions. Finally, we learn which questions are worth asking.'

Adapted

Educational leaders energise the planning and change process when they encourage vision, aspiration, a sense of mission, and an understanding of effectiveness. They encourage a positive disposition to change when they provide a description of future strategic horizons which makes sense in the day-to-day operations of the school and the team(s) they serve. They motivate towards change when they set out not to wrap up change within theoretical and abstract models, but when they work to put the desirability and benefits of a change initiative into the hearts of the people who will carry it out.

What means do individuals use to energise this process? Their planning is creative and systematic. It is:

◆ visionary – at both the preliminary and more definite stages; that is, regularly seeking answers to the questions – Where do we wish to be? Why? How? By when?;

◆ comparative – through analysing differences between the priorities as determined by the vision, with (a) the structure and achievement of the school now, and (b) the fitness of the staff to secure the goal;

◆ divergent – by involving different people and different types of expertise in the process;

◆ discursive – through encouraging open discussion and the brainstorming of different possibilities;

◆ strategic – by ensuring that initial and refined intentions are grounded in some form of prioritised development plan;

◆ disciplined – through setting in place an evaluation process and criteria by which to judge the success of the plan and the strategies in place.

Since change in the real world is multivariate, an essential beginning is to know and discuss what type of change(s) one is planning for and why. Thus ask yourself:

◆ Is the change a response to circumstances (for example, need to renew the school's image; need to respond to more student diversity; need to realign practices following revised budgeting; need to bring back order and purpose within an environment which has become destabilised)?

◆ Is the change a response to issues and recommendations arising from performance data (for example, inspection findings; outcomes of an audit; survey of staff, parents or students; the collation and examination of student achievement data; an overview of staff appraisals, or a probe into levels of student satisfaction)?

◆ Is the change to secure better practice (via more effective differentiation within teaching and learning; equity in the quality of practice between Key Stages; comparable levels of teaching and achievement across subjects and departments; improved use by the student body of self-study techniques, etc.)?

◆ Is the change a response to new technology (such as the wide-scale use of ICT in the learning process; membership of a virtual action zone; the introduction of new technical hardware and management information systems; revised professional development needs arising from the demands of using and responding to technological developments)?

◆ Is the change to secure compliance or accreditation (for example, retuning to meet legislative requirements or self-regulation goals; or to meet the requirements of institutionally-based accreditation – such as

Investors in People; Total Quality Management; National Charter Marks and Awards)?

◆ Is the change to give scope to creativity and the application of collective intelligence (empowering teamwork within the school; developing more flair in the manner and means by which the school goes about its business; setting up 'experience-exchange' projects with other schools; using ICT for broader networking and the extension of professional development activities)?

By going through the process of identifying the nature of the change, the school is establishing clarity about purpose and scope. It can also look across similarities and differences in the types of change to see if it is possible to forge links from one form of activity to another. In fact, a school could use these change dimensions or similar headings to 'map out' the full programme of innovation with which it is engaged, and then set down how this programme will be time-managed and resourced.

Whatever the nature of the change or its direction, the key to continuing success is to evolve and sustain the programme as a community challenge, not consistent threat. Equally, the processes to secure the change must not hinder creativity. This does not mean that strategies are vague and diffuse, just set off in the hope that they may possibly drift to a benefit, or merely left rooted in some kind of undirected programme of divergent thinking. The most productive type of creative process is to a large extent 'directed'. It is assisted by doing the following:

◆ reducing first stage complexity to a practical level of simplicity which resonates with 'what the school is about';
◆ choosing a strategic action which aligns well with and convinces the 'inner self';
◆ anticipating the actions and objections of the 'blockers' and examining ways to overcome such resistance;
◆ acting within an acceptance of ambiguity and confusion, rather than over-analysing an issue or task in the hope of starting 'error free';
◆ commencing with a leap of faith rather than looking for 'cast-iron' security or certainty;
◆ relaxing or refocusing any aspects of school procedures or culture which appear to hinder the creative process;
◆ establishing participative problem-solving teams;
◆ dispelling insecurities by promising and delivering a supportive structure to these teams;

◆ encouraging facilitation between participants, so that the process becomes a form of experiential learning, in preference to the agreement and transmission of formalised minutes or instructions;

◆ looking for small-stage 'early win' benefits and advertising these;

◆ ensuring that the chosen arenas of change and the creative processes underlying them do not become detached from the work of the school as a whole.

Energising the change process therefore is a multi-step approach. It arises from merging reflection with inspiration, direction, focused response and institutional learning. It includes rationality, but is more than just rational planning. It involves seeking to generate new ideas and working practices which may lie outside the general make-up and culture of the school. It is trying to open up differences in the thought pattern and in the planning and decision-making procedures.

Strategic PIN down – Reflection 6.2	**Aim**
	◆ to review 'team strengths' in relation to handling change and development.

In Table 6.2 are the beginnings of four lists. The items are selected from those usually listed as beneficial types of staff involvement in change. Complete the lists. Then find out which are strengths for you, or your team, or both. Tick those you feel competent with; mark in some way those you feel are not fully developed. Then complete the summary Table 6.3.

Table 6.2

Involvement	Decision-making	Action	Evaluation
Open meetings	Time to reflect and take stock	Workshops to develop skills	Performance data analysis meetings
Working parties	Brainstorming	Resource development	School self-evaluation projects
SMT – open door	Focused discussion	Team-based projects	Governor visits and reports
Staff-governor presentations	Multi-disciplinary work	Action research	Staff appraisal
Needs-based INSET	Being informed		Reciprocal observation
Regular briefings			Work sampling

Table 6.3

Summary table	Positives	Need development
Involvement		
Decision-making		
Action		
Evaluation		

6.4 Encouraging cross-disciplinary teamwork

Bits and Pieces

'No one can whistle a symphony. It takes an orchestra to play it.'

Subject expertise remains an important facet of a teacher's professional skill. This is recognised in the increased attention in recent years to ensuring that initial and later training gives adequate attention to subject knowledge and understanding. This importance is further reinforced by threshold assessment where one of the five standards is that teachers 'should demonstrate that they have thorough and up-to-date knowledge of the teaching of their subject(s) and take account of wider curriculum developments which are relevant to their work'.

Schools, of course, are not exclusively about subject matter and today few staff would consider their task to be solely the transmission of subject knowledge. The majority of teachers now accept the need to plan and teach co-operatively and to work collegially to ensure that their subject(s) interleaf with others in a manner which helps students to understand key concepts and apply core knowledge. The recent emphasis on 'key skills' has underpinned the need to ensure that all subjects contribute to crucial student competencies.

Identifying the part that a subject can play in the presentation of a cross-curricular project or theme, or in the development of a set of key concepts, is not onerous. Several schools already use curriculum guidance materials to help with 'mapping' exercises by which they determine which subjects will contribute what features and content. Equally, several schools now identify in their schemes of work links between subjects and how key skills are treated within subjects and across key stages. What is more difficult is ensuring that this curriculum structure is delivered.

'The challenge is to provide consistency, coherence and continuity. It is not enough to identify when topics touch upon cross-curricular

dimensions. Subject leaders must relate the engagement with the content to skill development. In this way teachers are encouraged to be "connective" as opposed to "insular" specialists.'

Field *et al.*, 2000

•

Interesting facts 6 The organisation and presentation of knowledge

How to value, organise and present knowledge has always been a controversial issue. Is the wisdom of the classical and intellectual philosopher of any more worth than the knowledge of the man and woman in the street? Are the ideas of artists, dramatists, historians, musicians and scientists, to name but a view intellectual domains, best represented through the content, conventions, symbolism, traditions and vocabulary of the separate academic disciplines which represent those domains? Is pure knowledge of higher intellectual worth than applied knowledge? How far is knowledge culturally determined and controlled, and how far should it be? Answers to these questions are neither clear-cut nor simple. Answers to them have varied across the decades and centuries, as has the opinion on whether or not students should be taught a subject-based curriculum or an integrated one.

The 1960s and 1970s saw some relaxing in schools of subject boundaries. Subject knowledge became more mixed at some age stages. There was a move towards exploring common concepts, and diversity in how to look from different academic perspectives at achieving planned, integrated project work. This corresponded to some degree with the moves from a status-bound hierarchical society where academic subjects were ranked as tightly as the subjects of the realm themselves, to a more open society where the insulation of different subjects and ideas from each other were challenged along with the 'anti-position' laid before many of the conventional authorities within society itself. By the late 1980s curriculum integration had been largely shed again and the National Curriculum was built around the 'ten winner subjects' with broad, thematic approaches relegated to the periphery of the weak and severely time constrained cross-curricular themes.

Now the pendulum appears to be swinging again and the organisation of the curriculum has been revised to represent ideas and concepts, which seemed on the very margins just a few years ago. Society is once again rather concerned that students should not just exit schools with specialist subject knowledge but with ideas on and commitment towards being good parents, responsible citizens and environmentally conscious members of the international community. In reality, the governing group in society wants both specialist subject knowledge and social environmental awareness.

That curricular aims, objectives and content should continually shift is to be expected for a number of reasons:

◆ first, knowledge is not a neutral commodity; it has always been seen as a source of power, even a dangerous thing, and there will always be a cry from some people that some types of knowledge should be confined to certain groups or individuals; approved knowledge does not occur in a vacuum, it is shaped, promoted, defended and protected in the context of the reigning social and political values;

◆ second, demonstrating knowledge in certain forms continues to be a type of social and career gate keeping and there are vested interests across many sections of society in keeping knowledge wrapped up, presented and tested in particular ways;

◆ third, knowledge can be used to develop the powers of thinking, so long as those powers don't develop to examine too deeply the values of the society that pays for the education in the first place; 'moral education' was a welcome addition to the school curriculum in the 1960s until some of the 'issues examined', ' the situations posed' and the 'proposed solutions' to problems were used by students to raise issues about society's double standards and the school's hidden curriculum – then some parents, some politicians and some teachers departed rapidly from the stance that moral education in the school curriculum was a good idea; (this is not to say that the materials used at the time to represent and present moral dilemmas were without fault – see the excellent review by Pring, 1984);

◆ fourth, knowledge and thinking are both reflective and retrospective, as well as conjectural and projecting; the school curriculum can be manipulated to control the degree of exposure that young people get to both types of intellectual analysis; just as the modern film-maker can adjust historical facts in favour of patriotic sentiment and box office receipts – so the politician, curriculum planner and teacher can control what young people learn in the classroom and whose version of events they examine; there really are those who hope you can fool 'most of the people all of the time'.

Thus, knowledge is precious, value-laden, politically and socially sensitive and teachers are not the only stakeholders in determining how it should be organised and presented and for what purposes. But if the school is an agency for cultural synthesis and curriculum development, education leaders must be willing to find their bearing in respect of where they stand on how subject expertise relates to wider competence, and what the school's role is as a mediator of tradition and culture. The challenge was well stated by Holt (1980):

> *'the curriculum must be seen neither as a seamless robe fashioned by the child from his own undirected experiences, nor as a patchwork quilt of separate subjects, each viewed as a distinct specialism without regard for a concept of general education. It must offer both unity and variety; it has shape and purpose yet it must provide a range of learning experiences which meet the varying responses of pupils and at the same time reflect an underlying rationale which can articulate them into a coherent whole.'*
>
> p. 53

An essential is to decide what common goals in respect of skills development the school is working towards. An equal essential is to determine the individual or team who will have responsibility to monitor if 'connections' are taking place and what coherence is present. Evaluative frameworks which distinguish between 'intended' and 'observed' outcomes can be most useful here. See, for example, Stake's (1976) ideas for examining the congruence between antecedents, transactions and outcomes, the Open University's (1980) approach to evaluating the central elements of classroom life, and the evaluation of teacher action plans in Hargreaves and Hopkins (1991). In general, consistency, coherence and continuity are more likely to be secured if:

◆ the nature of the collaborative project has been discussed and planned;
◆ the approach to controversial issues has been thought through;
◆ teachers have a clear understanding of the objectives;
◆ the objectives cover key skills and personal development;
◆ the projected timescale is clear;
◆ the chosen themes, topics and ideas closely relate to one another;
◆ the connecting points are well mapped and understood by all;
◆ what students will actually do and learn is overt;
◆ information is gathered about students' understanding and students' perspectives;
◆ there are regular meetings to assess progress against intentions.

Collaborative work involving cross-disciplinary considerations and actions, is more likely to be a creative process if there is acceptance that at many points it will be a fragmented and intuitive project. Development is by synthesis, including trial and error, it is rarely the implementation of a prescribed package. Creative networking in a larger school may need contributors to pass their distinct ideas and contributions into a 'cross-disciplinary' working party or similar – rather than have lots of information floating about from one subject or department to every other, i.e. A to B, A to C, etc. That is, the school sets up some kind of temporary or transient 'clearing house' which utilises and bonds all the different 'items', in order to avoid what might be overwhelming replication and overload.

To nurture creative ideas in this area of work, as elsewhere, it is necessary to have within the school:

◆ a non-threatening, supportive atmosphere to creative actions;
◆ activities which encourage the free flow of ideas;
◆ broad overlap in job descriptions and assigned tasks;
◆ a sequence to foster and develop aspects of team teaching, see Warwick's classical work (1971);
◆ different ways of pooling resources, teacher interests and the school's range of expertise;
◆ opportunities to re-examine long-cherished practices;
◆ a 'gardening' approach to development – roll up the sleeves, accept that everything will not stay clean and tidy, and work from the ground up;
◆ flexible use of those reward systems over which there is a measure of control.

Strategic PIN down – Reflection 6.3	Aims
	◆ to consider that communication, not technical know how, may determine whether a cross-disciplinary initiative makes it or not;
	◆ to select the target for an initiative and decide the range and pattern of communication.

Use Table 6.4 to plan a cross-disciplinary initiative.
1. Brief description of the initiative: themes, subjects / departments involved, key skills to be covered, core content, etc.
2. Communication matrix

Strategic PIN down – Reflection 6.3 cont.

Table 6.4

Key question	Response
With whom will it be necessary to communicate?	
What will be the nature of the communication?	
When will the communication happen?	
Where will it happen?	
For what purpose?	
How will the communication be sustained, reported and evaluated?	

Issues in focus 6.3

Field *et al.* (2000) state that the purpose of a communication will determine the most appropriate type or combination of types to be used, or the style of communication – for example, it is difficult to motivate colleagues via letters or memos or to negotiate via e-mail (although not impossible – everything depends on getting the tone right).

In looking at the effectiveness of communication, leaders may want to ask the following questions:

1   *What are the objectives of the communication?*
    Being clear about what needs to be achieved and spelling out exactly what has to be done is important. It might be worth asking if the communication is necessary.

2   *What are the purposes of any specific communication within the team?*
    Purposes can include informing colleagues about a particular event or development, getting a team member to perform a task, obtaining information from colleagues, seeking views as part of a consultation, trying to convince others of a particular idea or action, and praising achievements and performance.

3   *Is the communication clear, unambiguous and concise?*
    The leader may want to check that the communication matches the purposes and objectives, and that any message is not open to misinterpretation. Most messages need to be brief and to the point – rambling prose is not usually welcomed.

4　*Is the communication addressed to the appropriate people?*
Is the communication for one member of the team or for all? If others outside of the team need to know, how will they be informed?

5　*Are the style and type of communication appropriate?*
It is worth considering whether a brief chat might be more productive than a short note or memo, whether a meeting will be the most efficient means of achieving specific objectives. Balancing formal and informal communications, and ensuring the styles of communication are appropriate can contribute towards effective leadership. Particular thought needs to be given to the type of communications which go to staff and others via students.

6　*Is the communication being sent at the most appropriate time?*
Putting off communications can result in missed opportunities and additional pressures. In most cases, messages are best delivered at the same time decisions are made.

7　*Is the communication being sent to the correct location?*
It may seem obvious, but it is worth checking which is the most appropriate location – home, pigeon hole in school, by hand or by e-mail.

8　*How will you know if the necessary action has been taken?*
The leader may need to establish procedures to check if the communication has been acted upon and whether any feedback is required. For a very important communiqué, remember to 'check, double-check and re-check'.

6.5　Nurturing school-based action research

Emerson　　'We aim above the mark to hit the mark.'

Action research tries to establish simultaneous links between improving practice and improving understanding. It dates back to the forties and the introduction by Lewin (1947) of community-based investigative/ development projects in the USA. The concept was developed extensively in education in England in the 1970s and 1980s by pragmatic curriculum innovators and researchers such as Stenhouse (1979) and Elliot (1981).

Generally speaking, this type of research has the following constituent elements:

◆ the principles and methods of research are applied to practical situations or practical issues;

◆ there is a developmental approach – seeking to empirically justify and lay the foundations for change;

◆ the research is planned and 'owned' by the school (or consortia);

◆ it follows a survey, planning, action, monitoring, revised action, sequence;

◆ it involves practitioners in examining features of their work and gathering evidence of its impact;

◆ it usually involves both observation and reflection;

◆ it is replicable – i.e. capable of being carried out by other schools or other teachers;

◆ it ties in decision-making with objective evidence, particularly feedback from the classroom and the life and work of the school;

◆ it approaches fact finding from a structured and organised perspective.

The key features of action-research have been described by a number of advocates – for example, Cohen and Mannion (1980), Kemmis *et al.* (1981) and Hitchcock and Hughes (1995). Kemmis *et al.* describe the process in the following way:

> '*It ... begins with a general idea that some kind of improvement or change is desirable. In deciding just where to begin in making improvements, one decides on a field of action ... It is a decision on where it is possible to have an impact. The general idea prompts a "reconnaissance" of the circumstances of the field, and fact-finding about them. Having decided on the field and made a preliminary reconnaissance, the action researcher decides on a general plan of action. Breaking the general plan into achievable steps, the action researcher settles on the first action step. Before taking this first step the action researcher becomes more circumspect, and devises a way of monitoring the effects of the first action step. When it is possible to maintain fact-finding by monitoring the action, the first step is taken. As the first step is implemented, new data starts coming in and the effect of the action can be described and evaluated. The general plan is then revised in the light of the new information about the field of action and the second action step can be planned along with appropriate monitoring procedures. The second action step is then implemented, monitored and evaluated; and the spiral of action, monitoring and replanning continues.*'* p. 2

Though some aspects of action research now tend to be multi-stage rather than cumulatively single stage, schools will recognise the cyclical nature of the process and some will have experience of applying it to curriculum innovations and the development of school-based review. Overall, the research has to be conscientiously undertaken and the findings publicly shared. Although 'ownership' is one of the big advantages and motivating influences of action research, external perspectives and/or moderation of findings by others can act as safeguards and prevent the research from becoming just 'insider collusion' (Lomax, 1994)

Running in parallel with the use of action research as a form of educational development was the idea of the teacher as 'extended professional' (Hoyle, 1980) and Stenhouse's (1979) concept of 'teacher as researcher'. Both ideas were grounded on the premise that to be effective practitioners, teachers also needed to be reflective scholars and research-based investigators – principally by combining day-to-day practice in the classroom and school with a strong commitment to professional development and the use of forms of systematic enquiry. More recently, the Teacher Training Agency (1996) has revived the idea of 'teacher-as-researcher' through its promotion of teaching as a research-based profession.

> *'Although there is much to be done to bring teaching and research closer together, there should be no difficulty in principle – for teaching and research are based upon closely related skills and concerns.'*

TTA, 1996, p. 2

All of these ideas incorporate the notion of 'enquiry and reflection' as being a central part of teachers' professionalism. The application of these skills should be to both classroom and the institution as a whole. The outcomes should benefit students, school development and professional learning. In essence, it is an expectation that teachers can build upon what is known about their area of specialism, while maintaining their commitment to teaching responsibilities. They can do so by combining robust research methods with classroom practice. The advantages of these approaches are the recognition given to wider professional opportunities and the capacity for professional collaboration. The downside is that unless such involvement is carefully considered, planned for and supported with any additional training which is needed, the general efficacy of both the school and teachers' work may diminish. Additionally, the 'field of action' may be very limited, given the ever-increasing central control of the curriculum, teaching time and teaching method.

Whatever the risks or limitations may be however, action research and the role of 'teacher as researcher' provide platforms from which to begin journeys of participation and collaboration which have the potential to engage teachers' interests in the development of learning and the educational change process. School leadership needs to encourage what facets of such enquiry it can put in place, and through it seek to promote teachers' evaluation and development of their own practice. This is more likely to happen if:

◆ the work is placed within the staff development programme and linked with some form of accreditation;
◆ there is a range of 'research-based activity' which offers different opportunities for involvement or permits different levels of contribution, thereby allowing teachers to participate in line with their interests, expertise, and professional commitments;
◆ the range of investigations undertaken is based on shared perspectives and negotiated priorities;
◆ the projects are suitably scaled and manageable;
◆ the knowledge and skills needed to make a worthwhile contribution to research are audited and enhanced;
◆ the work is supported by external consultation and/or facilitation whenever possible;
◆ the research done is utilised and linked with other school development activities;
◆ the work is genuinely part of the school's culture and not some special 'one-off' which is then forgotten;
◆ the conclusions are context-specific and framed to suit the reality of existing time and resources;
◆ those who make a substantial contribution to the research are part of the dissemination team;
◆ whenever possible, the work involves governors, parents and students in an active sense and not just as a 'captive audience of subjects' – there for interview, survey and investigation.
◆ the leadership itself models facets of research-based activity and 'learns alongside colleagues.'

Issues in focus 6.4

Reed and Learmonth (2000) propose that it is helpful to make a distinction between school improvement that is *shallow* and that which is *deep*. They see both types to be of importance and to be fit for different purposes. While shallow can concentrate on short-term measures and specific outcome-based investigations, deep school improvement looks to answer more difficult questions and to deal with influences on practice from within and outside the school. The latter approach also seeks to investigate in more depth the intricacy of the full teaching and learning process. Ideally, any research-based activity would incorporate the evaluation and development of both types of improvement, but the deeper work is more likely to extend teachers' critical and evaluative skills.

In the final analysis, school-based research or school-based investigation of any kind needs to be approached with optimism, imagination and a sense of humility. We are making the best of what is available, not changing the world at a single stroke. The research should be framed so that others can pick it up and carry on. The most important aspect may be the very questions we decide to ask.

> 'Techniques are to be learned, but they can answer only the questions which we have the imagination to ask ... the most important stage ... is the stage at which you sit down to ask what we really want to know ... If we ask dull questions we shall get dull answers; if the question is not strictly relevant to our theoretical or practical needs, the answers will not be useful ... imagination coupled with a strict passion for logical argument, is also what makes for a good report.'

Sapsford,
1999, p. 247

Strategic PIN down – Reflection 6.4

Aim

♦ to think through and answer important questions about developing and evaluating a piece of action-based research.

Complete the following worksheet:

A   What is to be the *point of focus*? Teaching techniques; impact of an aspect of work on a particular year group or type of need; evaluating the impact of policy; the use of key skills across the school; the effectiveness of staff decision-making; students and parents perceptions of homework, etc.

Strategic PIN down – Reflection 6.4

B   How is this *focus justified*? Response to inspection findings; agreed area of need; determined after student-shadowing; follow-up to request from students or parents; insights from a programme of school self-review, etc.

C   What *criteria* will you use to evaluate the success of the research?

D   What *information, skills and techniques* will the team use to (a) carry out the research; (b) communicate with each other; and (c) provide feedback to colleagues and the school as a whole?

E   How will governors, staff, students and parents be *informed* about (a) the research and its purposes; and (b) the outcomes and impact?

F   What measures will be taken to ensure the research is *cost-effective*?

G   How will the research *contribute to forward planning*?

H/I/J School to add and answer three of its own questions.

6.6   Summary

> 'To teach is to learn twice.'

Joubert

◆ Conviction underpins commitment.

◆ Commitment is sharpened when leadership demonstrates its words in actions.

◆ The maintenance of morale and commitment is one of a leader's daily tasks.

◆ Change requires vision to be welded to day-to-day issues and presented in a manner which speaks to the individual's heart and imagination.

◆ Students need the curriculum to be 'connected.' Opportunities for teachers to discuss and work alongside each other are the building blocks of this connection.

◆ Formalised opportunities for systematic reflection on practice provides potential links between teaching and research. The potential of 'teacher-as-researcher' is that it combines professional practice with enhanced professional learning.

'Progress is the realisation of utopias.' Oscar Wilde

No matter how school leadership is arranged and the level at which individual teachers lead, there is a need to look at oneself honestly and objectively in order to deduce what personal development is necessary to 'grow and develop' in the job. From the start, however, it has to be recognised that any team or individual analysis involves risks. Self-reflection may encourage and inspire if one can identify and concentrate on steps achieved, tasks well done, positive feedback received and teamwork well carried out. But a self-review may equally point up ideals not met, goals not secured, an image not as one might hope, and, perhaps, weaker personal characteristics than one thought before the mantle of leadership was acquired. To maintain a balanced perspective, it may be helpful to accept that in practice the potential of one person or one team is never fully realised. The challenge is to maintain momentum, to continue to meet daily difficulties, to seek the ever forward road, and in so doing, to increase personal and team maturity. Through confronting fears, self-illusion and defensiveness – one may be strengthened rather than reduced.

Clearly, it is not helpful to undertake any type of self-analysis if one over-relies on personal 'moods of the moment' or impressionistic perceptions of self-worth. There is scope to introduce a degree of objectivity in the process, perhaps by compiling a list of key questions about the function of leadership and then working through them as a kind of self-review – concentrating on the *professional role in practice*, not on self-worth as a person. The questions might include the following;

- ◆ Is my brief understood by all who need to know? If there are gaps, how do I best explain the brief?
- ◆ Is the brief rooted in educational values and what is significant for students? Are these beliefs communicated widely?
- ◆ Is there balance in the brief between maintenance of the administrative functions of leadership, the inspirational aspects of leadership, and the development of leadership as a response to staff, students and to new school activities?
- ◆ Am I creating/contributing to a school culture in which improvements to teaching and learning are central?

◆ Is my sense of vision for the school/team and school/team tasks unrealistic for now or about right?

◆ Given my brief as it stands, and the 'best fit' picture of how it might change and develop – what skills do I apply well?; what skills do I need to refine or acquire?

◆ How am I sharing the leadership task? Can I share it more?

◆ Who are my colleagues with positive attitudes to our programme of change? Am I networking with them to best effect? How can we spread our joint influence?

◆ Does my use of time reflect my public pronouncements? Am I walking the talk? Am I being what I want others to be?

◆ Do I encourage all to take a share of celebration and blame – or do I take too much on myself?

◆ Do I find places where I can dream and recharge? Do I encourage others to?

Notice board 12 What staff say about what makes successful leadership

◆ Clear and consistent values.

◆ Keeps others informed.

◆ Easy to talk to.

◆ Fair and consistent.

◆ Relays clear instructions.

◆ Is not aloof but does not try to be 'one of the group'.

◆ Takes time to listen.

◆ Presents confidence and self-assurance.

◆ Picks up signals from staff and situations.

◆ Not reluctant to take charge when necessary.

◆ Cool and calm most of the time.

◆ Seeks to develop co-operative relationships and structures.

◆ Demands consistency but not conformity – recognises different ways to the goal.

◆ Empathises with the team's problems.

◆ Shows personal honesty – leading to respect.

◆ Demonstrates flexibility/tolerance.

◆ Projects excitement/adventure about the work.

◆ Bats for the team and represents the team through the good and bad times.

◆ Gives clear feedback – looks for the positive, but does not ignore the need.

◆ Has appropriate professional knowledge – willing to pass it on.

◆ Understands the broad issues and new trends.

◆ Maintains consistent standards of expectation.

◆ Enforces agreed procedures and discipline.

◆ Good at troubleshooting.

◆ Takes share of cover and 'filling in'.

◆ Effective with organisation and paperwork – gives attention to detail, when needed.

> **Notice board 12 What staff say about what makes successful leadership cont.**
>
> ◆ Takes deadlines seriously.
>
> ◆ Recognises best efforts and praises good work.
>
> ◆ Thinks it's important to keep colleagues happy.
>
> ◆ Empowers other staff – trusts colleagues and will delegate.
>
> These characteristics may be used for self- or team review
>
> Adapted from various sources

Remember that leadership is not a certain path but the art of making the best of the journey. You need to inspire but you also need to be inspired. Turning aspirations or dreams into a sense of direction and encouraging staff to respond are no easy matter. It takes consistency and commitment and arises from many different applications of leadership. The most significant contributions are a personal belief in a corporate purpose for the school as a whole, coupled with the investment of energy towards securing it. The presentation of the vision has to be seen as substance, not just image and style. The primary focus needs to be the people end of the equation. Time spent in persuading them to come on board and to contribute different talents, has the potential to turn leadership itself into a collective endeavour. In this complex world this is surely the way to go. Educational leaders need to muster all the support they can find.

> *'No matter how deep a study you make of it, what you really have to rely on is your own intuition and when it comes down to it, you really don't know what is going to happen until you do it.'*
>
> Matsushita

Adair, J. *Effective Teambuilding*, London, Pan Books, 1986.

Adair, J. *Effective Leadership Masterclass,* London, Pan Books, 1997.

Ainscow, M., Hopkins, D., Southworth, G. and West, M. *Creating the Conditions for School Improvement*, London, David Fulton, 1996.

Alimo-Metcalfe, B. 'An investigation of female and male constructs of leadership and empowerment', *Women in Management Review* 10(2), 1995, pp. 3–8.

Audit Commission *Towards Better Management of Secondary Education*. London, HMSO, 1986.

Banks, O. *Parity and Prestige in English Secondary Education*, London, Routledge, 1955.

Barker, A. *Making Meetings Work,* London, Industrial Society, 1993.

Barr, L. and Barr, N. *The Leadership Equation*, Oxford, Oxford Psychologists Press, 1989.

Barth, R.S. *Improving Schools from Within,* San Francisco, Jossey-Bass, 1990.

Bass, B.M. and Avolio, B.J. *Improving Organisational Effectiveness Through Transformational Leadership,* London, Sage, 1994.

Berne, E. *Games People Play: The Psychology of Human Relationships,* London, Grove Press, 1964.

Boyatzis, R. *The Competent Manager,* Chichester, Wiley, 1982.

Brathay Conference Report *The Leadership Odyssey*, Cumbria, Brathay Hall Trust, 1998.

Brighouse, T. and Woods, D. *How to Improve your School,* London, Routledge, 1999.

Brown, E. *Loss, Change and Grief: An Educational Perspective,* London, David Fulton, 1999.

Chang, R.Y. and Curtin, M.J. *Succeeding as a Self-Managed Team,* London, Kogan Page, 1994.

Civil, J. *Leadership Skills for Success,* London, Ward Lock, 1997.

Cohen, L. and Mannion, C. *Research Methods in Education,* London, Croom Helm, 1980.

Cooper, C. *Surviving at Work,* London, Health Education Authority, 1995.

Cox, T., Boot, T. and Cox, S. 'Stress in schools: a problem-solving approach', M. Cole and S. Walker (eds), *Teaching and Stress,* Milton Keynes, Open University Press, 1989.

Department of Education and Science *Teacher Education and Training,* (James Report), London, HMSO, 1972.

References

DfEE *Excellence in Schools,* London, DfEE, 1997.

DfEE *Gaining the NPQH: Guide for Applicants,* London, DfEE, 1999.

DfEE *Professional Development Support for Teaching and Learning,* consultation paper, London, DfEE, 2000.

DfEE/QCA *Education for Citizenship and the Teaching of Democracy in Schools,* London, QCA Publications, 1998.

Dukes, J.A. *Assessing Management People: A Practical Guide,* London, Routledge, 1988.

Elliot, J. *Action-Research: A Framework for Self-Evaluation,* Cambridge, Cambridge Institute of Education (mimeograph), 1981.

Everard, K B. and Morris, G. *Effective School Management,* London, Paul Chapman, 1990.

Evetts, J. *Becoming a Secondary Headteacher,* London, Cassell, 1994.

Fidler, B. *Strategic Planning for School Improvement,* London, Financial Times/Pitman, 1996.

Field, K., Holden, P. and Lawlor, H. *Effective Subject Leadership,* London, Routledge, 2000.

Forbat, G. 'Bumpy ride', *Times Educational Supplement,* 28 April 2000.

Ford, C. M. 'Creativity is a mystery', C.M. Ford and D.A. Gioia (eds), *Creative Actions in Organizations,* London, Sage, 1995.

Garwood, M. and Dowden, M. *Curriculum Management and Assessment Manual,* London, Pearson Education, 1999.

Garratt, B. *The Learning Organization,* London, HarperCollins, 1994.

Gronn, P. *The Making of Educational Leaders,* London, Cassell, 1999.

Hammond, P. 'The HoD's survival guide (performance management)', *Managing Schools Today,* March 2000.

Hardie, B. *Evaluating the Primary School,* Northcote House, 1995.

Hargreaves, D.H. and Hopkins, D. *The Empowered School,* London, Cassell, 1991.

Hay McBer *Raising Achievement in Our Schools: Models of Excellence,* London, Hay Group, 2000.

Herzberg, F. *The Motivation to Work,* New York, John Wiley and Sons, 1959.

Hitchcock, G. and Hughes, D. *Research and the Teacher,* 2nd edn, London, Routledge, 1995.

Holt, M. *Schools and Curriculum Change,* New York, McGraw-Hill, 1980.

Honey, P. *Solving People-Problems,* New York, McGraw-Hill, 1980.

Hoyle, E. 'Professionalisation and deprofessionalisation in education', in Hoyle, E. and Megarry, J. (eds) *World Yearbook of Education 1980: Professional Development of Teachers,* London, Kogan Page, 1980.

Katzenbach, J.R. and Smith, D.K. *The Wisdom of Teams,* Boston: Harvard Business Press, 1993.

Kelly, G.A. *The Psychology of Personal Constructs,* New York, Norton, 1955.

Kemmis, S. *et al. The Action Research Planner,* Victoria, Deakin University Press, 1981.

Kline, P. *Personality: The Psychometric View,* London, Routledge, 1993.

Lawlor, H. *Effective Leadership in Schools: An Overview,* CELSI Occasional Paper No.1. Canterbury Christ Church University College, 1999.

Lawlor, H. and Sills, P. 'Successful leadership – evidence from highly effective headteachers', *Improving Schools,* 2(2), 1999, pp. 53-60.

Lawlor. H. and Sills, P. 'School leadership: towards greater understanding and effectiveness'. Forthcoming in *Improving Schools,* 2000.

Leigh, A. *Perfect Decisions,* London, Arrow Business Books, 1993.

Leithwood, K.A. 'The principal's role in teacher development', in B. Joyce (ed.), *Changing School Culture through Staff Development,* Alexandria, VA, 1990.

Levacia (eds), *Improving Educational Management Through Research and Consultancy,* London, Paul Chapman Publishing, 1994.

Lewin, K. 'Action research and minority problems', *Journal of Social Issues 2,* 1947.

LMI *LMI Industry Reports* November round up, 1999.

Lomax, P. 'Action research for managing change', N. Bennet, R. Glatter and R. *Improving Educational Management Through Research and Consultancy,* London, Paul Chapman Publishing, 1994.

Macbeath, J., Boyd, B., Rand, J. and Bell, S. *Schools Speak For Themselves,* London, NUT, 1997.

Macbeath, J. *Effective School Leadership,* London, Paul Chapman Publishing, 1998.

Macbeath, J. *Schools Must Speak for Themselves: The Case for School Self-Evaluation,* London, Routledge, 1999.

Marland, M. (ed.) *School Management Skills,* London, Heinemann, 1988.

Maslow, A. *Towards a Psychology of Being,* Van Nostrand Reinhold, 1968.

McCall, C. *School Self-Review Manual,* London, Financial Times/Pitman Publishing, 1998.

McGregor, D. *The Human Side of Enterprise,* New York, McGraw-Hill, 1960.

McLaughlin, C. 'Stress factors – taking control', I. Craig (ed.), *Managing Primary Classrooms,* London, Pitman Publishing, 1997.

McLelland, D.C. 'Testing for competence rather than intelligence', *American Psychologist* 28(1), 1973.

Mischel, W. *Personality and Assessment,* Chichester, Wiley, 1968.

References

National Commission for Education *Success Against the Odds,* London. Routledge, 1996.

O'Brien, P. *Taking the Macho out of Management,* London, Sheldon Business Books, 1993.

OFSTED *Improving Schools,* London, HMSO, 1994.

OFSTED *Planning Improvement: Schools' Post-inspection Action Plans,* London, HMSO, 1995a.

OFSTED *Guidance on the Inspection of Secondary Schools,* London, HMSO, 1995b.

OFSTED *Standards and Quality in Education (1998–1999),* London, The Stationery Office, 1999.

O'Neill, J. 'Whose job is it anyway?: The team leader as catalyst for management development', *Educational Management and Administration* 23(1), 1995, pp. 19–27.

Parry, G. *Coping with Crises,* London, BPS and Routledge, 1990.

Peters, T. and Austin, N. *A Passion for Excellence,* London, Guild Publishing, 1985.

Pring, R. *Personal and Social Education in the Curriculum,* London, Hodder and Stoughton, 1984.

Reed, J. and Learmonth, J. 'Revitalising teachers' accountability: learning about learning as a renewed focus for school improvement', paper presented to 13th International Congress for School Effectiveness and Improvement. Hong Kong, 2000.

Rosener, J. B. 'Ways women lead', *Harvard Business Review* Nov./Dec.. 1990.

Sapsford, R. *Survey Research*, London, Sage Publications, 1999.

Schmuck, R.A., Runkel, P.J., Saturen, S.L., Martell, R.T. and Derr, C.B. *The Handbook of Organisation Development in Schools,* Palo Alto, CA, Mayfield Publishing Company, 1972.

Scott, J. and Rochester, A. *Effective Management Skills: Managing People,* London, Sphere Books in association with the British Institute of Management, 1984.

Sergiovanni, T. *Leadership for the Schoolhouse,* San Francisco, Jossey-Bass, 1996.

Smith, N.I. and Ainsworth, M. *Managing for Innovation,* London, Mercury Business Books, 1989.

Stake, R.E. *Evaluating Educational Outcomes,* Paris, OECD, 1976.

Stenhouse, L. 'What is action-research?', Norwich, CARE University of East Anglia (mimeograph), 1979.

Stow, D. *The Training System,* Glasgow, 1840.

Tannenbaum, R. and Schmidt, W.H. 'How to choose a leadership pattern', *Harvard Business Review* 36(2), 1973, pp. 95–101.

Thody, A. *Leadership of Schools: Chief Executives in Education,* London, Cassell, 1997.

TTA *Teaching as a Research-based Profession,* London, Teacher Training Agency, 1996.

TTA *National Standards for Headteachers,* London, Teacher Training Agency, 1998.

Tuckman, D.W. 'Development sequence in small groups', *Psychological Bulletin* 63(6), 1965, pp. 384–399.

Warwick, D. *Team Teaching*, London, University of London Press, 1971.

West-Burnham, J. and O'Sullivan, F. *Leadership and Professional Development in Schools,* London, Financial Times/Pitman Publishing, 1998.

Whitty, G. 'Teacher professionalism in new times', paper presented to the Annual Conference of the Standing Committee for the Education and Training of Teachers, Rugby, November 1999.

Wilcox, B. *Time-Constrained Evaluation,* London, Routledge, 1992.

Willms, J.D. *Monitoring School Performance,* London, The Falmer Press, 1992.